ROCK *doesn't* ROLL
on an empty stomach

Stories and recipes from a rockin' cook's journey fueling
America's biggest touring bands
of the 70s and 80s.

With kitchen-tested recipes used
in my thirty years of catering.

Midge Trubey

All attempts have been made to preserve the stories of the events, locales and conversations contained in this collection as the author remembers them. The author reserves the right to have changed the names of individuals and places if necessary and may have changed some identifying characteristics and details such as physical properties, occupations, and places of residence in order to maintain their anonymity.

Cover design by St. Petersburg Press and Isa Crosta
Cover Photograph by Christopher D. James
Paperback ISBN: 978-1-940300-33-7
eBook ISBN: 978-1-940300-34-4

First Edition

Contents

Entertainers We Fed

AC/DC

Adam Ant

Air Supply

Al Di Meola

Alice Cooper

The Allman Brothers Band

Arlo Guthrie

Atlanta Rhythm Section

B-52s

Bar Kays

Barbara Mandrell

Barry Manilow

BB King

The Beach Boys

Beastie Boys

Bertie Higgins

Bill Washington, Dimensions Entertainment

Billy Crystal

Billy Idol

Billy Joel

Black Sabbath

Blackfoot

Blondie

Blue Oyster Cult

Bob Dylan

Bob Marley, Jr.

Bob Seger

Bruce Hornsby

Bruce Jenner and Linda Thompson

Bruce Springsteen

Butterfly McQueen

C.K. Spurlock

Cab Calloway

Carol Burnett

Chaka Khan

Charlie Daniels Band

Cheap Trick

Chicago

Chuck Mangione

Climax Blues Band

The Commodores

Crystal Gayle

Danny Joe Brown

Dave and Sugar

Dave Brubeck

The Dazz Band

Dee Clark

Dennis Nyback

Devo

The Diamonds

Dick Cavett

Dionne Warwick

Dire Straits

Donna Summer

Donny and Marie Osmond

Dottie West

The Drifters

Duran Duran

The Eagles

Earl Klugh

Eddie Money

Edwin Starr

Emerson, Lake and Palmer

Emmylou Harris

The Emotions

Eric Clapton

Fabian

The Fix

Flock of Seagulls

Forrest Tucker

The Four Tops

Frank Marino &
Mahogany Rush

Gallagher

The Gap Band

Gary Proper, Jack Link
and Associates

George Benson

Gino Vannelli

Gladys Knight
and The Pips

Glenda Jackson

The Go-Go's

Gordon Lightfoot

Grace Slick

Graham Nash

Grover Washington, Jr.

Hall and Oates

Hank Williams, Jr.

Harry Chapin

Heart

Henry Paul Band

Herbie Hancock

Hootie and the
Blowfish

Humble Pie

The Irish Rovers

Isaac Hayes

The Isley Brothers

The J. Geils Band

Jack Link and
Associates

The Jackson Five

James Garner

James Taylor

Jan and Dean

Jeffrey Osborne

Jerry Corbetta

Jimmy Buffett

Joe Jackson

Joe Lambusta, Magic
Productions

John Davidson

John Denver

John McLaughlin

John Prine

John Stoll, Fantasma
Productions

John Waite

Johnny Mathis

Jon Valentino,
Fantasma Productions

Journey

Kansas

Katherine and Robert
Altman

Keep the Fire

Ken Kragen

Kenny Loggins

Kenny Rogers

Kim Carnes

The Knack

Kool and The Gang

Larry "Bud" Melman

Larry Gatlin

Lauren Bacall

Leif Garrett

Leon Russell

The Lettermen

Liberace

Little Anthony

Little River Band

Los Lobos

Lou Rawls

Loverboy

Luther Vandross

Marvin Gaye

Maynard Ferguson

Maze

Men at Work

Merle Haggard

Michael Jackson

Michael Landon

Mike Pinera

Millie Jackson

Missing Persons

Midge Trubey

7

Molly Hatchet

Mothers Finest

Mr. Mister

Neil Sedaka

The O'Jays

The Outlaws

Ozzy Osbourne

Parliament Funkadelics

Pat Metheny

Pat Travers

Patti Smith

Paul Anka

Paul Dooley

Pete Rivera

Peter Tosh

The Police

The Pretenders

Prince

Ray Charles

Ready for the World

REM

Renaissance

REO Speedwagon

Rick James

Robert and Kathryn Altman

Robert Palmer

Robin Trower

Rod Stewart

The Romantics

Ronnie Montrose

Roy Buchanan

Roy Clark

Rufus

Rush

Sam and Dave

Sha Na Na

The Shirelles

Sly and the Family Stone

Smokey Robinson

Southside Johnny and The Asbury Jukes

Spyro Gyra

Star Castle

Starship

Steve Smith and Vital Information

Stray Cats

Supertramp

Sylvia Porter

Ted Nugent

Teddy Pendergrass

Ten Years After

Ten Years Later

Thin Lizzy

This Is It

Thompson Twins

Tina Marie

Tom Chapin

Toto

Triumph

Turning Point

Utopia

Van Halen

Weird Al Yankovic

Whitesnake

Willie Nelson & Family

Yes

ZZ Top

I first met Midge when I joined the Kenny Rogers tour. There was a small army of performers, crew and drivers and Midge's catering room was always a happy place. All day long Midge served up meals and smiles to everyone before packing up, driving to the next venue and doing it all over again.

At the beginning of the tour I found out I was pregnant with my first child. Midge took extra care of me and always had ice cream in the freezer for my after-show cravings. It didn't take long for us to become friends for life. Love you Midge.

Crystal Gayle

Crystal Gayle and Husband Bill Gatzemos circa 1979

The author with Crystal Gayle, Melanie Dooley, Crystal's husband Bill Gatzemos

How it All Began

It was raining cats and dogs. I drove my old boat of a Cadillac convertible through a parking lot at Eckerd College. Tearing over the grass and curbs, I pulled right up to the classroom door of the building where famed economist and author Sylvia Porter was going to speak. You see, I had just picked Sylvia up from the beauty salon. She couldn't get her hair wet, could she?

The year was 1977, and I truly felt like I had it all. I had a husband whom I loved, plus I had two wonderful children. Melanie was 6 years old, and Corbett was one. I helped my husband at his family business and was busy myself with the two children and doing volunteer work with the Junior League of St. Petersburg, Florida. Life was good, life was full.

A very dear friend of mine, and fellow Junior League member, called and asked me to co-chair the Free Institution Forum program with Eckerd College in St. Petersburg. Top name speakers were brought in from all over the country, and Sylvia Porter was scheduled for this event. Sylvia's money articles were in all the newspapers, and she had several bestselling books on the charts. Whenever there was a survey of the "top ten women in the country," Sylvia was listed. I was thrilled to be able to meet such a commanding woman. My job was to pick her up at the airport, get her to her hotel, help her with any personal arrangements, and assist her with any requests she might have while in St. Petersburg. I was totally thrilled to be co-chairing this event. She arrived with one of her best friends in tow, stating that she never booked speaking engagements but had decided to take this one since she needed something new to do as she had just lost her husband.

I enjoyed working with Sylvia all week. I helped her get her favorite scotch (Johnny Walker Red) for her hotel room, get her to her hair appointment, and get her to and from all her speaking engagements (without getting wet).

The day arrived when I was taking her back to the airport. She thanked me for taking such good care of her and told me how very much she appreciated my efforts.

I replied "Surely you receive this kind of assistance wherever you go. You're one of the most admired women in the United States!"

"My dear," she said, "usually I am given a map, keys to a car, my per diem money, and then I am on my own."

"I just cannot believe my ears!" I exclaimed.

But she verified that was usually the case. I felt that someone of her stature should be shown extra courtesies, not just left to be on their own. This was the less-than-a-minute conversation that changed my life forever. This conversation was the birth of my idea for the Personal Touch, my career.

We parted ways, vowing to keep in touch. I am very proud to say that we did until the day she died. I was able to express my gratitude to her both by telephone and by letter for this life-changing experience. Sylvia wrote that she was gratified to have helped another woman succeed in business. Her letters to me are some of my most-cherished possessions.

A few nights later, I was riding my bicycle with my husband, Dennis, jogging beside me. I relayed my Sylvia Porter conversation to him as the wheels in my brain started to turn. I decided that I was going to do some research in our community to find out what happened when high-profile people came to visit the Tampa Bay area. My burning questions: Could they find the services that they needed to make their visit pleasurable? Did they know where to go for the best restaurants that the area had to offer? Did they know where to shop if they had unlimited funds? Did they need babysitters for children? Did they fall in love with my hometown? Then, the thought occurred to me that these people were so high profile that they could not go out to eat at a restaurant without being interrupted by the adoring public. Was it possible for them to eat out at all?

I began my investigations. I went to hotels. I talked to limousine drivers, and I went to the two arena managers in St. Petersburg and Tampa. I found that there was no one locally that could be contacted to be of assistance to such individuals when they were traveling through the Tampa Bay area. These high-profile people traveled with their own personal assistants who would scramble to find what was needed in each city or town. The arenas had no kitchens. Here was a person or group that had all kinds of money for food but no time to go out to eat. I thought maybe there is a place for me! Maybe someone would hire me to help them with filling their local needs, even cooking. Then the thought occurred to me: if my idea really took off, my husband and I would have our own business. He wanted out of his family business, and maybe this could be the way for us to have our own business.

After months of talking to anybody that would talk with me, I went to my girlfriend's carrying all my notes. While she babysat my children, I wrote out my first little brochure. I called another friend of mine, gave her a copy of my brochure, and asked her to help me name the company. In about a week, I received a great list of ideas for names. On that list was "The Personal Touch," and my company name was born.

My next step was to visit with my father, an attorney, and ask for his advice. I thought my father was going to pass out at the thought of what I wanted to undertake. His daughter, who he had sent to college, which he paid for, a sorority girl, wanted to embark on a totally out-of-the-box business. My liability exposure scared him to death. My idea was not normal for a "girl" that was raising a family; this was not a hobby. I wanted to start my own business. Remember, this was 1977.

At first my father was not sure that this idea of mine would even take off, but he wanted to make sure that I was legal and filed the papers with the state. My next step was to go to a printing company to pick out a company color. The printer told me that all the companies were using red and black ink. Red and black just did not work for me. I wanted Kelly green, which has always been one of my most favorite colors and the color of money, which was why I was in business. I was told that printing would take longer as green would need a special run of the press. My next stop was a t-shirt company picking out a Kelly-green shirt and having "The Personal Touch" printed in white on the front, with my name printed on the back.

Next to the City of St. Petersburg to get a license to do business. The City of St. Petersburg did not know what to do with me. The girl at the counter called Tallahassee, the capitol of Florida, to see what kind of a license they should issue. Tallahassee told the local office that there was no one license that encompassed all the services that I wanted to offer; therefore, I was issued a "personal servicing" license. I thought my father was going to choke, and I did not dare tell my mother.

I went to all the people that I had talked with previously, taking my brochure and all the confidence I could muster to push my brainchild. The Personal Touch was to encompass the traveling person's need for shopping, babysitting, local directions, entertainment – with cooking thrown in as an option. I did not have to wait very long for the telephone to ring. Approximately six weeks after I peddled my brochures, I received my first contract, and my company was born. The most surprising element was that the only service the person at the other end of the telephone wanted was a home-cooked meal.

I come from a large family that was always cooking. My grandmother, mother, and mother in law were terrific cooks. Thank goodness I had learned from them throughout the years. I was not afraid of the kitchen. As a matter of fact, I knew I could hold my own in the kitchen under pressure.

Trial by Fire

That first call came from a concert promoter that liked the idea of a home-cooked meal on the road.

My first contract was July 24, 1977 at Curtis Hixon Hall in Tampa, Florida for the Isley Brothers.

Are you kidding me? The great Isley Brothers wanted me to cook for them?!

I was too excited to be scared to death. Wow! Someone actually wanted me to cook for them!

The Isley Brothers

The Isley Brothers were such a hot group during this time, particularly for me personally. Back in high school in the Sixties, I had danced to "This Old Heart of Mine," "Shout," and "Twist and Shout." Who during this era had not wildly thrown their arms up in the air proclaiming "Shout!" while trying to dislocate every back vertebra and pull every muscle? In college, the song "It's Your Thing" was at the top of the charts. I can remember being so excited in 1967 when I was invited to the Homecoming of VMI (Virginia Military Institute) and, the added bonus was The Isley Brothers were playing for the big formal! I boogied myself stupid; I loved to dance. When I got my first contract, and it was The Isley Brothers, all those past memories came flooding back. The Isley Brothers were popular in the Seventies, and today they are true legends and still making music.

The one big problem at that time was Curtis Hixon Hall did not have a kitchen. Little did I realize at the time, but very few concert arenas in the country had kitchens at all. Food was usually ordered through a local restaurant or caterer, put into a Styrofoam container, and delivered to the side of the stage. The food sat in that little box until someone picked it up to eat it. Sometimes hours would pass before the food was consumed. Imagine how disgusting that sitting food tasted!

The big question was, how was I going to pull this off? Proper planning was a must. What Curtis Hixon considered a kitchen was a big room with some metal counters on one side of the room and one deep sink with running water. There was an ice machine on one side of the room. That was a big plus because as I would soon learn, the ice machines were sometimes on the other side of the building.

Midge Trubey

I had to make my own kitchen. Tables and chairs were no problem as each facility had those readily available. Ice was available at each concert in huge ice machines. Electric power existed as long as you knew where to find the circuit breakers. My logical approach was to load picnic coolers with food, purchase electric fry pans and fifth burners, buy a portable barbeque grill, get some beverage containers, and I would be all set. What man did not like a salad, mashed potatoes, and a fresh-cooked steak off the grill for dinner?

To say that this was simplistic is indeed an understatement. When I received a copy of that first contract and saw all the items that the promoter wanted me to provide, I was a tad perplexed. I was suddenly initiated into the world of contract riders for the bands. A rider is the non-technical portion of the contract where the band makes personal requests with the local promoter producing the concert. These requests become part of the contract and must be provided to keep the contract valid. These riders were always a nuisance to the promoters who were primarily interested in promoting the shows and having increased ticket sales. A band's personal requests were an annoyance to the big picture of concert production. It became crystal clear to me how much these individuals wanted to have their favorite items from home provided for them while they were traveling across the country. The catering riders were to become my specialty and my business.

Of course, breakfast, lunch, dinner, and the dressing-room set ups were on the contract. The one item that I was not prepared for was to provide towels for the dressing room. Towels?

I had to find a way to add bath towels and all the other dressing room requirements to my list of duties. I had never thought of that! Guys need sweat towels and towels to take showers. I learned early on that no building at that time wanted to provide towels since they were always taken at the end of the night onto the tour buses, never to be seen again. Towels were a real pain to keep track of. Well, yours truly did not have this knowledge at the time, so I added towels to my list. I quickly grabbed the yellow pages and found a towel outlet in upper Pinellas County. I called the store and made arrangements to drive up county to pick them up. I wish I could remember the price of towels at that time. I do remember putting the entire cost of the towels on the bill as a rental just in case I did not get them back. Bingo! If I got them back, I could wash them and use them again. After each concert, I ran around backstage looking for those white towels, like Easter eggs, all over the place. Each towel I found was extra money in my pocket, and the buildings were very glad not to be in the towel business.

Did I tell you before that I had no fear? I must have said to myself a thousand times, "You can do this. How hard can it be?" Well, I was about to be initiated into the world of rock-and-roll.

No stove to cook with and no refrigerator; what to do? Microwaves were just coming out. No one on the road trusted microwaves, but I did not know that on my first show. I planned on fixing good ol' meatloaf with real mashed potatoes and some steamed vegetables. A big salad, bakery rolls with butter, and a yummy dessert finished my first dinner menu. This menu was approved by the promoter. I knew that I could fix meatloaf in my microwave that I was taking from my house.

I struggled with the pricing. I ran to the grocery store to get shelf prices, then ran back home. How much was my time worth? I knew that I could not lose money; I just wanted to see how my ideas would work in theory. I had to at least break even. I figured if I was onto something, I would get better with my pricing as time went on. If time went on. My husband and I did not have extra money to be throwing around.

I will tell you this: I never lost money on any show, not even these first few shows. I always made money from the very beginning. I picked up extra money at each concert for extra add-on requests. These ranged from a specific candy bar to a special soda or extra beer for the buses. These extras had not been expected, but I learned early on to be ready for them.

Here it was, my first concert, and the problems that I encountered made a long list. The first problem was the weight of the microwave. Oh, my goodness, trying to get it into my Volkswagen van almost killed me! I pulled all the utensils, pots, and pans that I needed from my own kitchen at home. The fact that I was cooking dinner for 30-40 people did not bother me. I also had to locate disposable trays for the deli trays, vegetable trays, and fruit trays that I would have to make on site. Everything had to be done on site; I was being hired to cook. Next, I had to find some type of containers to put all the beverages in that I was to provide. The list included beer, juices, sodas, gallons of bottled water, and bottles of sparkling water like Perrier. I would buy new trash cans, put the beverages in them, and fill them with ice from the hall. I had to make soup for lunch. Well, go buy a fifth burner, put your pot on it and make the best soup anyone had ever tasted, but not out of the can. The soup would be made from scratch. When I was finished with the soup, I would use that same burner to make my mashed potatoes. Oops, I need to buy another burner to cook the vegetables. Oh yes, don't forget to take the family toaster I needed for breakfast. I learned early on that there was never enough coffee backstage. Buying two large coffee makers was the first major equipment purchase that I had to make. I grabbed my tea kettle off my stove to make hot tea for the dressing rooms as I loaded my van.

I wanted my food tables to look appealing. The guys were used to food in Styrofoam containers, prepackaged, and being left at the edge of the stage. I loved the look of red and white checkered table coverings; they looked so clean and happy. I bought a big roll of it from a carnival store to go on all the tables -- this had not been done before. Oh, yes, I loved flowers. What to do? Flowers were not part of the contract budget. Remember I told you that I was a thrifty gal? Well, I called my aunt who was in all the garden clubs all over town. What could I do for no money? My aunt had the answer. Her best friend owned a funeral home, and they always had flowers that no one wanted. I know that

Midge with first back stage room table

this sounds so weird, but I called him and went to pick up some big bouquets that were left over. I took all the flowers out of their containers and put them in my own vases. Ta-da! Now I had flowers to go on the food tables and in the dressing rooms. Casual flowers like this had never been provided backstage, particularly on all the food tables. The flowers were eye catching and made my red and white checks look so cheerful. I agree that if anyone at the time had known where the flowers came from, they would not have been as popular as they were. I really think everyone would have been grossed out! All the guys always loved my flowers in these beginning days. Flowers on the food tables were to become my standard look throughout my rock n roll catering days, flowers from the grocery store. Now the secret is out as to where I first got my flowers in my hometown.

Trial by Fire

It was physically impossible to prepare the food on site for breakfast, lunch and dinner, cook the food, clean up and set up the dressing rooms all by myself. Who could I get to help me? My darling sisters were the answer. My sister, Alice, became my strongest supporter, working with me throughout every project for the entire 30 years of my business. Alice always worked full time for a large company, but she always found time to help me on many a project. She used a large portion of her vacation time helping her older sister. My sister, Carol, worked around her schedule helping me for the first few months. I was truly blessed to have had these two darling gals that always believed in their older sister. At this time, my other sister, Robin, was raising her children that were the same age as mine. Many years later, Robin was employed by my company--as was everyone in my family: cousins, nieces, nephews, and even my Dad at one point.

On the night before my first concert, the van was loaded with equipment, but what about the food? I set my alarm clock for early in the morning, kissed my husband goodbye for the day, and took off for the grocery store. I loaded my van with the groceries that I had put on my list (I checked my list until it was all crumbled), threw the groceries in the van, and chugged off to Curtis Hixon. Ok, now that I had the groceries, everything fresh from the store, what was I going to do with them once I got to Tampa? Remember, they did not have refrigeration. Well, my darling Daddy was a big camper. I borrowed every cooler he owned, plus I got every cooler that my husband and I had in our garage. That was going to have to do, certainly during the day as I rotated all the food with the meals. I would be fine, right? Believe me, I was a nervous wreck. My darling sisters met me in Tampa. They believed I could do anything, God bless them. We all took a big deep breath and started our first workday.

Looking the part was a big plus. I had jerseys made up with my company name on the front and our personal names on the back. We wore jeans and sneakers. We were three girls that were not bad looking. We were willing to provide a great breakfast/lunch combination, a good dinner, and have the dressing rooms set up on time and looking good. The hall had provided the tables and chairs for the men to eat their meals. Each dressing room had one eight-foot table in it for the food for each group. For this first meal, all utensils and plates were disposable which was a tremendous plus for me at these beginning concerts. I was to find out very soon that most groups wanted dinner to be provided with china and flatware, but I am getting ahead of myself.

I wish I could embellish this part of my story with something terrible that went wrong or that I could remember something truly awful happening as the day progressed, but this was not the case. My sisters and I just chugged along all day with our plan. My sisters did everything that I asked them to do. Word leaked out around dinner time that this was the first show that I had ever done. The road manager came running up with a look of panic asking me if this was true. I have to say, I do not like panic or trauma, and that was written all over his face. I must tell you, I told him a little white lie. I told him that it was my first show there at Curtis Hixon. I do remember him saying something like "thank God." He was not in the mood to have anything go wrong with such a prestigious show. Yew! I dodged that big bullet. I told my sisters to quit telling everyone that this was our first show. The girls were so excited. They did not know their chatter was causing concern.

As I was setting up the dressing room for the Isleys, I met a man named "Gorgeous" George O'Dell. Everyone called him "Gorgeous George", and I will never forget that name. He was just so nice. He told me he was impressed with the set up and our performance that day. He asked for one of my business cards informing me that his brother "Hotdog" was one of the managers on tour with The Commodores. He told me he was going to call his brother when he got to the hotel and in turn, have his brother call me to handle the food for the Commodores when they came into St. Petersburg two weeks later. I just about fainted with excitement. The Commodores! They were so hot on the charts. Not to mention, I loved their music. I thanked him in advance, not believing my good fortune. Gorgeous George gave me such confidence and encouragement.

The day finally ended later than we expected, but there we were, three happy girls loading all our equipment back into the van. We knew that night that I had a winner with my concept of the Personal Touch. The men had been beside themselves with compliments. They loved the food but told me not to use the microwave again as they believed "nuking food" was unsafe. (Again, times have changed.) They loved the set up and the care that we had provided in cooking their food and setting up the dressing rooms. They were impressed that the food had been fixed on site, it was fresh, and it had been served to them on the buffet by a smiling face. I was beyond thrilled.

The concert that night was beyond anything that I had ever experienced. I had never been backstage before. The men let me up on stage to watch some of the show, hidden behind one of the giant speakers. Wow, memories of high school and college dances came flooding back. I could not help but dance with my baby sisters, hidden from view. The lights, the sound, the music -- I was hooked.

Something told me I had not seen the last of Gorgeous George, and I was hoping to hear from Hotdog.

The manager at Curtis Hixon had believed in my business concept in my planning stages. He was so supportive that when he received reports on how well everything had gone back stage with the Isley Brothers, he was willing to continue recommending me to the promoters bringing shows into his hall. As I was to learn early on, a smooth show makes for great public relations for everyone involved: bands, promoters, concert halls and crew. Everyone wants to have a good experience, especially when the workdays are long. I was about to learn just how long and hard those days could be.

Supertramp

My second show was also at Curtis Hixon. I had been contacted about this show before the Isley Brothers appeared on my calendar. The concert was Supertramp, July 30, 1977. Less than one week after my first concert, along came concert Number Two.

The music of Supertramp was creative, jazzy, and very big on the music charts. With catchy tunes like The Logical Song and Give A Little Bit, this show was another sell-out performance like the Isley Brothers. My services caught their promoter's attention as the members of this band were big vegetarians and, at the time, being a vegetarian was totally not understood. The prior complaints from the band were that they were getting celery sticks and carrot sticks with dip for dinner, and nothing well rounded. When the promoter first contacted me, I was enthused. My father in law was a vegetarian, so I was very used to what a vegetarian was and how to prepare interesting dishes. The well-known promoter decided to give me a try because I knew about vegetarian food. The promoter had a great reputation and was extremely nervous trying someone new.

I came clanking into the hall again with bags of groceries, coolers, towels, pots, pans, and burners, but this time, I had a vegetable steamer and a rice steamer with me. It was common sense to me that the food needed to be fresh. I picked up the steamer for the rice at a natural food store. How come no one had ever done this before, I asked myself? Remember at this time, all these special rices we take for granted today were not on the shelves of the grocery stores. I had gotten special juices from this same health food store. My sisters again were there to help me. This promoter was never a

Midge Trubey

19

calm person backstage, constantly asking if all was OK, and wanting to go over the schedule for the millionth time, adding stress to our day. After working for this promoter for many years, "nervous" was constant period. Our lucky stars were on our side again; the day went so very well. The guys, John Anthony, Roger, Rick, Bob, and Dougie were pleased with the day. They loved their freshly-steamed rices, vegetables, and fresh fruits. Hurrah!

Supertramp was so popular at the time that a few months later, the Personal Touch was asked to travel with them to Miami to do a concert and be at the Bayfront Center in St. Petersburg the following day. This meant back-to-back days of concerts in different cities, something I had not tried before. At this time, I was still developing the where's and how's of getting from town to town to fill the contracts that we were given. I had the bright idea that we needed a motor home so that my gals traveling with me could sleep during the night while I drove. I thought I could work all day and drive all night. I was more concerned about the stamina of my girls than myself. Well, here lies the story. Coming up from Miami, the rented motor home blew its engine. There we were on the Florida turnpike, engine smoking, and stopped at the side of the road. The motor home had a CB, so I began calling like crazy for any help I could find. I told my girls to go to sleep because someone had to. Another motor home pulls up and who should get out? Roger Hodgson, the keyboard player of Supertramp! I was never so glad to see anyone in my life. His wife had just had a baby, and they were sleeping in his motor home. Roger's driver had heard my frantic calls on the CB

My sisters, Alice and Carol at our first ever concert

and directed him to pull over to help us. I had never rented a motor home before, so I had no idea what to do or how to do it; this was big trouble. Roger took over completely to help us. As we were waiting on one of those truck mechanics, I told Roger he should go on down the road as he had precious cargo, plus he was Supertramp. He needed his sleep also. He was looking forward to getting to St. Petersburg as his sister lived in the county. He was excited about introducing his brand-new baby to his sister. Roger would not leave me. He went into his motor home, brewed a pot of Morning Thunder tea, and we sat together waiting for a mechanic to show up. I will never forget his kindness that night. When I told him it was more important for him to get sleep, he reminded me that it was just as important for me as I was an important part of the show. The guys needed me. Wow, that was the first time I had ever really been told that. After many more cups of Morning Thunder, the mechanic showed up and managed to fix the rented motor home, then our two motor homes went barreling into St. Petersburg. Roger insisted on staying with me in case the motor home broke down again.

My sister, Alice, was meeting me at the Bayfront Center so I could get some sleep and to help with the set up. Well, come set up time, no Midge. She was frantic and the promoter was not too pleased either. The only way that I had to contact them was the CB, and between Roger's motor home and mine, we reached the truckers pulling ahead of us into the Bayfront Center. The message was "The Chuck Wagon is coming. She is on her way." Alice put the coffee on for the men. We started a little late in St. Petersburg, but the day went well. The day before in Miami had gone well also. I think the promoter calmed down when the word got out that Roger was with me, and that I had truly broken down on the road. That night when the band sang Take the Long Way Home, John dedicated the song to me. My Breakfast in America signed album looks like it has been through World War III, but I am totally proud of the fact that the entire band signed this album. John was always a big joker; he signed it "You can personally touch me up anytime." I remember yelling at him, "how am I going to take this album home?" My children would read it someday, not to mention my husband. How scandalous! Even during this early time, I considered myself a Mom and a friend, but never a girlfriend. The jokes of my "new brothers" and "road family" had started.

My sister Alice, heading to the dressing room for clean up

Midge Trubey

Frances' posh squash

2 lbs yellow squash (about 6 cups). combine squash with zucchini, if desired

1 c mayo

1 c parmesan cheese, grated

1 small onion, chopped

2 eggs, beaten

½ tsp salt

¼ tsp pepper

½ c breadcrumbs

1 tbsp butter, melted

Preheat oven to 350 degrees.

Cook squash in boiling water for 5 minutes. Drain well and pat dry in strainer.

In a mixing bowl, combine mayo, parmesan cheese, onion, eggs, salt, and pepper, stirring well to mix thoroughly.

Add squash and stir gently. Pour into lightly-greased 1.5 quart casserole dish.

Mix the breadcrumbs and melted butter, then sprinkle on top of squash mixture. Bake at 350° for 30 minutes.

Zucchini Recipe From My College Days

This is a recipe I saved from one of my debutante parties when I was a deb so many years ago.

– Serves 12 –

6 lbs medium-sized zucchini

¼ c Cream French salad dressing

2 tbsp prepared mustard

¼ cbutter, melted

1 c dried breadcrumbs

1 tsp dried basil

1 tsp salt

Preheat oven to 350 degrees.

Wash zucchini to make sure all dirt is removed. Cut off ends and drop whole into boiling water. Cook until tender, usually 10 minutes.

Drain, cut in half lengthwise, and place flat side up in a buttered baking dish.

Stir together salad dressing and mustard; spread on zucchini.

Mix the remaining ingredients and sprinkle on top. Bake uncovered 350° for 20 minutes.

Midge Trubey

Alice's Broccoli Salad

I have friends asking me to bring this one to picnics all the time!

Salad

1 head Broccoli, use florets only, cut into bite-size pieces

8 slices cooked bacon, crumbled

½ c red onion, chopped

½ c golden raisins

8 oz shredded sharp cheese

½ c cherry tomatoes, halved

salt & pepper to taste

Dressing

2 tbsp white vinegar

¼ c sugar or sugar substitute (Splenda blends the best)

1 c mayonnaise (Hellmann's or Dukes)

Combine salad ingredients in large bowl.

In a separate bowl, whisk together dressing ingredients. Pour over salad and mix well.

Refrigerate and serve.

Wild Rice Salad With French Sherry Dressing

Gorgeous in color, plus so yummy for a vegetarian dish. Pair with Sherry French Dressing below.

– Serves 8 –

∞∞

Salad

3 c Cooked wild rice, straight or blend of brown/ wild rice (must be completely cool)

2 tbsp scallions, sliced, including green tops

8 cherry tomatoes, halved

18 oz can artichoke hearts, halved

1 c frozen green peas

2 tbsp parsley, chopped

1 dash garlic powder

salt and pepper to taste

French Sherry Dressing
(makes 5 cups)

1 egg

1 tsp sugar

2 tsp salt

4 c salad oil (can use 2 cups salad oil and 2 cups olive oil)

½ c apple cider vinegar

½ c sherry (not cream sherry)

2 garlic cloves, barely crushed

∞∞

Thaw frozen green peas under hot water. Drain and pat dry.

Add all salad ingredients into mixing bowl.

In your blender, mix egg, sugar, and salt together. Add oils and vinegar, alternating until all oil is used, then drip in sherry slowly. Place in a jar with tight fitting lid, add the barely crushed garlic cloves, so they can be removed from the jar before the dressing is poured on to your salad.

Midge Trubey

This dressing should be stored in the refrigerator until ready to use.

Keep separate from your salad until ready to use.

Your salad can be stored in the refrigerator also until ready to use.

Before serving, take salad out of fridge and let sit until room temperature. Stir the salad well before you dress it. Shake dressing until combined, then remove then garlic and pour over salad to taste, you will not use all of the dressing.

Will store safely in the refrigerator for up to one week.

The Commodores

My business was off to a great start! I learned right away that a smile and a kind disposition went a long way. Try not to look like the deer in the headlights, try to think on your feet, and keep smiling all the time. Being helpful was also a big plus, as long as whatever you were asked to help with did not interfere with your main purpose for being backstage. The concert days are action packed with lots of responsibilities, and everyone must pull their weight.

Gorgeous George did not disappoint me. He kept his promise about having his brother call me. A few days before the Supertramp concert, my telephone rang, and it was Hotdog. He was traveling with the Commodores. Gorgeous George had given him great reports about our food and service. The Commodores with the Emotions were playing The Bayfront Center on August 6, and Hotdog wanted to hire us for the concert. I was beyond thrilled. In a period of less than two weeks, I had been given the opportunity to showcase my new business with three of the top bands in the country. The Commodores were beyond hot. They were on fire with such tunes as Slippery When Wet, Fancy Dancer, Just to Be Close to You, High on Sunshine, Easy, and Brick House. They were the top rhythm and blues group in the country. They had crossed all lines of music with disco, funk, pop, and of course soul. The band members were Milan Williams on keyboards, Thomas McClary on lead guitar, Ronald LaPread on bass, Walter Orange on drums, William King on trumpet, and last but not least, Lionel Richie, singer and song writer. The band always put on a great stage show with dance moves and flashy stage clothes.

As I talked with Hotdog about what the band required and what dinner menu would make them happy, the subject of good ol' southern BBQ came front and center. Regular breakfast and lunch were fine, but BBQ was their favorite, so could I do that? I learned very early that when a client has a special request, the answer is always, "Yes, no problem." If the client cannot see your smiling face, then your voice better be smiling over the telephone.

When I got off the phone, I knew at this time period, there was only one person in St. Petersburg that I could call to help me with the best BBQ that anyone could ever get. I have always felt that in business, you do not have to reinvent the wheel. If there is someone that excels in a certain area, that is the person you should call to help you or to give you advice.

Without hesitation, I picked up the telephone book to call Big Tim of Big Tim's BBQ. I had been eating Big Tim's BBQ since I was a little girl when he had a shack back off one of the main roads. My dad used to go get his BBQ to bring home to the family. I called Tim during regular business hours and was told that I would need to talk with him personally, so I should come to the restaurant that night. Dennis, my husband, babysat the children, and I got in my car to go meet the famous Big Tim.

When I showed up at the appointed time to talk with him about helping me with the dinner menu for The Commodores, I was told that I had to go out back behind the woodshed to meet with him. I have to say, I was a little timid. Well, around the corner I went to this very dark parking lot and at the far end was the smoker shed. I started yelling out "Big Tim, Big Tim, it's Midge Trubey, you told me to come and meet you." From behind the shadows emerged one of the biggest men I have ever seen, I mean, solid, tall, with muscles everywhere. He asked who I was, and when he was satisfied that I was who I said I was, he broke out into a big grin and extended his hand. He told me that the front counter people thought I was an undercover cop. He apologized for startling me, but he made it clear, that he would not have come out of the shadows if I had not been who I said I was. As I stood there talking to Tim about my new business and my contract with The Commodores, all uneasiness disappeared between the two of us. He agreed that he would provide the BBQ ribs, chicken baked beans, coleslaw, BBQ sauces, and bread and butter. I also ordered his sweet potato and pecan pies, which were just fabulous. We shook hands to seal the deal. I knew that with Tim's BBQ, my service, and providing the rest of the contract, I could not go wrong. I felt like I had a winner before the concert day arrived.

Concert morning and afternoon proceeded without a hitch. The set up and backstage crew at the Bayfront Center were just as nice as the Curtis Hixon crews. The road crew of the Commodores was very friendly, plus I finally got to meet Hotdog. By show day, I had talked with him on the telephone several times, so it was like meeting an old friend in the flesh. As sound check approached, the Commodores entered the building. What a great bunch of guys. Also, the opening group, the three darling sisters who made up the Emotions came into the building.

The Emotions were very interested in the business I was creating; even their daddy, who was their manager, had encouragement for me. Their Rejoice album was in the top ten at that time. "Best of My Love" was their top song. I appreciated their encouragement but really loved their music too!

As dinner time rolled around, I met Big Tim at the backstage door at the appointed time. He was right on time. My tables were set up

The Commodores

with lots of color and flowers, and then in comes this fabulous BBQ feast. The crew ate in one area, and the band ate in an adjoining room. Everyone was laughing, talking, and loving the food. The sweet potato and pecan pies were a big hit. I also had a big bowl of fresh cut fruit that was a hit. I will never forget this scene as long as I live. When the band finished eating dinner, all of them literally rolled out of their chairs onto the carpeted floor groaning "how are we going to play tonight?" They lay there for at least a half an hour trying to get their dinner to settle before getting into their stage clothes. When you are stepping over their bodies cleaning up the tables, you learn a lot about those people, and they learn a lot about you. The men said that normally they would never eat that heavy because of all the dancing that was in the show, but they just couldn't help themselves. The Commodores also told me that I had a hit in the manner in which I was doing business; they thought the concept was a winner. I was on cloud nine! The men waited as long as they could to get into their stage costumes, remaining flat on the floor as long as possible.

The Bayfront Center had a unique backstage area that gave certain people a unique vantage point to watch the show. You could stand one floor up from the stage at the back of the hall overlooking the back of the stage. You could see over the speakers, giving you a great view of the band and all their dancing. Oh, my goodness, did I dance that night! I had a lot to dance about as my talks with the Commodores and the Emotions had been so uplifting. I went home more convinced than ever that the Personal Touch could grow into a good, solid business. I was one happy woman.

This was not the last time that I worked for the Commodores before Lionel went out on his own. The next time I worked with them in concert, something very special happened to me, something I have never forgotten. I was again standing at my usual vantage point backstage at the Bayfront Center, and Lionel saw me dancing

Note written by me to take home to my daughter, Melanie. The Emotions for Melanie

Midge Trubey

up there. He began singing to the crowd Three Times a Lady. My unforgettable moment came when Lionel actually came around to the back of the stage looking up at me and finished singing the song. He looked right at me and gave me a low bow. To this day, when I hear that song, I tell whoever is around that Lionel Ritchie sang that song to me all those many years ago. That was a big moment in time for me. Lionel Ritchie is an icon in this crazy music business. He will never know what a thrill he gave this woman back in 1978 (that was the next tour through Florida). I actually have the little photograph of Lionel coming back up from his bow and blowing a kiss to me. Wow! I still have it; talk about an impact.

From August to November 1977, I didn't have any concerts, but I was working on getting my name out in the industry. There was a lot going on in my personal life at this point. My husband, Dennis, had decided to leave his family music business and took a job outside of Chicago. He was supposed to train for his new job in Illinois until the spring. After training, he would be assigned his position somewhere in the country, but we had no idea where. We had just enrolled our little daughter, Melanie, into kindergarten. Corbett was just toddling around.

Lionel Richie coming up from his bow after acknowledging me watch him from backstage

I did not think it would be a good move to drag the children to Chicago for the winter and change Melanie's school, plus my business was just getting off the ground. I also thought that I was building a business for the two of us to run. Dennis had other plans. Looking back on it now I realize that this was a critical time in our marriage. I don't think either one of us realized that the decisions we were making were going to cost us our marriage a little further down the road. Hindsight is 20/20.

Midge's Favorite Baked Ham & Glaze

◇◇

Most of us (by now) have our own favorite way to "Bake A Ham." My favorite way truly depends on the moods of my Gemini Twins!

I use ham, usually Smithfield, whole or half

Put into baking pan with lots of room fat side up. Score the fat. Dot the fat with whole cloves stick them in there. Then rub your ham with good ol' yellow mustard, then pack your ham with brown sugar (I use light brown). Then take canned pineapple rings and toothpick them into your ham and pick a cherry in the middle. Take your pineapple juice from the can and pour into the bottom of your baking pan. (Sometimes, my twin will add OJ to the pineapple juice). Do sprinkle the top of your pineapple slices with a little more brown sugar.

Put your ham into the oven to bake as directed on ham cooking instructions. The last hour of baking your ham, baste your ham with all the juices from the bottom of your pan. Above all else, do not over bake your ham!!! IF you overcook your ham, cut your ham to display on a pretty platter than use the juices from the pan on top to rehydrate your ham (last resort).

◇◇

Midge Trubey

Sweet Potato Casserole

A huge hit any time of year, not just the holidays.

– Serves 6-8 –

◇◇◇

Butter to grease baking dish

1 c firmly packed light brown sugar

1 c chopped pecans

½ c self-rising flour

½ c butter, melted

3 c mashed canned sweet potatoes

½ c granulated sugar

1 c sweetened flaked coconut

½ c raisins

2 large eggs, lightly beaten

1 tsp vanilla extract

¼ c heavy cream

◇◇◇

Grease your casserole dish. For the topping, in a medium bowl, stir together brown sugar, nuts, flour and ¼ cup melted butter (half of what you have made), set aside. In a large mixing bowl, stir together potatoes, granulated sugar, coconut, raisins, eggs, vanilla extract and the remainder ¼ melted butter. Stir in cream, combining well. Spoon into prepared casserole dish. Spread topping over sweet potato mixture and bake at 350° until golden brown, 20-30 minutes.

More Than Just Food

I could never have accomplished this great journey without the support of my family. My mother was totally horrified that I was going to be backstage with "people that had such horrible reputations." She read all the newspapers and was convinced that I would have terrible personal problems being involved with "such people". In actuality, I was a very protected woman backstage, sometimes having my own security guard.

My mother was extremely southern and figured nothing of any good would take place backstage. My reputation as a lady of good upbringing would be destroyed. As a past debutante, the career I was embarking on was totally unacceptable.

I had never been backstage at a concert in my life before my first contract. Up to this point of my life, I had only attended a handful of concerts. I loved music and had always enjoyed music of all kinds, even as a child. But after college, I was married, and the extra money for attending concerts was not available.

When the children were born, the radio was my constant companion around the house and in the car. I loved to dance and sing (singing is something I am requested not to do), so my love of music was always there. It was extremely exciting to me to become involved in the making of the music that entertained so many people, including myself. I had never dreamed that I would meet the people that made the music that I so loved. To be involved with the production of such live concerts was a position that I never would have thought possible. But here I was, being asked to cook food for the entertainers that the world loved. I was also entering a male-dominated field back in 1977; I did not have a clue.

When you are cooking for people, it is extremely personal. Think about it. What do you like for breakfast, lunch, dinner? What do you want for your dressing room for food and beverages that make you comfortable? What do you need to stay healthy? Who is traveling with you -- family, friends, new baby? All of these questions are a normal concern for the traveling person, but back in 1977, it was not even considered on the level that it is today.

I was ahead of my time with a human approach to people that were as normal as you and I. Granted, some were not as normal, but that is human nature for each of us to be different from one another. We are not all alike, and when so much money is involved, your perspective

Midge Trubey

33

does change. My initial premise in dealing with my entertainers was we all put our pants on the same way each day, we work in the same place, so let's make today as pleasant as possible.

My job was to provide each group with a home cooked meal on location, be on time, follow directions, and be flexible if the day should blow up. A day could easily be sidetracked if the sound was not perfect or if the lighting did not work. The technical production became something that I truly admired - these geniuses of technical electronics. Believe me, an army of rock n rollers travels on their stomach, the same as any army. Food is essential for anyone to have a productive workday. When you are working in a different city each day, and you have only had a few hours of sleep, food becomes critical to your wellbeing.

Emerson, Lake and Palmer

My fourth contract to provide food backstage was for Emerson, Lake and Palmer -- ELP as they were called in those days. The concert was November 27, 1977 at the Bayfront Center. These men were not only hot on the charts, but were hot looking. You had Carl Palmer on the drums, Keith Emerson on keyboards, and Greg Lake on guitar and vocals. They were known as a classy group of men. Their music was again different from the other groups that I had worked for. Their music was classical, jazzy, and rock with a little touch of Americana thrown in. I was thrilled to be able to have contact with such a high-profile group.

I made sure that I had done my homework with my contract, made my lists, and checked them twice. The day went off again without a hitch. This is truly the beginning of a story of great association with the men as a group and individually.

The staging of this show was tremendous for the time period. The beginning of the show was a mind blower. As Fanfare for the Common Man played, the stage was lit with blinding white lights and pyrotechnics coming from the back of the stage. The floor opened up, and you saw Greg, Keith, and Carl's silhouettes coming up from beneath the stage. At first you could only see their heads, and the crowd screamed louder as the men continued to walk up the underground stairs to the stage level. As their forms got larger, the crowd was in a frenzy, all the time Fanfare was blaring. By the time the men got to their instruments, the audience was hysterical. I still get goose bumps thinking about that opening. Carl was known as one of the top-rated drummers of his time. He could make those drums reach your very soul. Keith was a trained concert pianist and organist; he could get every emotion out of those keyboards. Greg, as the front man, had stage presence with a winning smile that drove the ladies crazy, plus his vocals were outstanding. Their music was different from the standard rock n roll of the day. To say they had a huge following in those days is an understatement. Lucky Man was written by Greg. The words to this song should be listened to again for our day and time; the words still apply. Other songs include C'est La Vie, From the Beginning, and Karn Evil 9. These titles are some of their greatest hits. Wow, what a show. I don't think the crowd ever sat down.

As I was cleaning up backstage after the show, I got summoned to the front office because the tour manager wanted to talk with me. My vision of a perfect day of work immediately disappeared. I was scared that I had done something wrong. What was the reason I was being called in to the office? When I walked in, my heart sank. At the conference table sat the promoter and the production manager of the show. I sat down before my knees gave way.

My initial fears were immediately put to rest as the ELP production manager told me the entire group had been very impressed with my service that day. He had a special request of me, if I could handle it. His younger brother, Bobby, who was the assistant production manager, and his girlfriend, Suzanne, wanted to get married the next day, Monday, here in St. Petersburg. Bobby and Suzanne had applied for their Florida marriage license at the show in Jacksonville a few days before. He was sending a jet to Jacksonville to pick up the marriage license first thing in the morning. He wanted his brother to have a real ceremony with the traditional reception. Was this something I could help him with? I did not hesitate; the answer was yes. I was a St. Pete girl, and I figured I had all the resources to accomplish the task. Ted then told me to go back to work backstage and meet up with him in an hour at the bar in the Hilton across the street from the Bayfront Center. Here he would give me the specifics of what he wanted to do for his brother.

As I left the meeting, my excitement was greater than my fear of failure. The challenge was a rush. I ran to the payphone to call my babysitter to let her know I was going to be home later than expected. Dennis had already gone to Chicago.

Having to go to the Hilton for this meeting initiated me into the private life of super stars -- a big eye opener for this mother of two. The hour was past midnight, around 1:00 am. Big bodyguards stood at the entrance to the elevators going up to the floors of the hotel. If you were staying there, you had to show a key. The bar was completely closed unless you were on the guest list. I said to myself, guest list, what guest list? I told the security guards my name. I was on the list, and I was permitted to enter the elevator and go to the top floor, which was the bar. As I entered, the place was packed. I recognized the men that I had fed that day as I pushed through to find the groom's brother for my meeting. He was sitting at a table with some of the guys, but no chair for me. I sat cross legged on the floor at his feet, notebook in my lap, to get my instructions for the wedding for his brother. Holy cow, what had I gotten myself into as I furiously took notes?

The jet was flying to Jacksonville early that same morning to pick up the marriage license. He wanted his brother to have a full church wedding with a minister officiating. Keith would play the organ. The bride was wearing a grey dress, and flowers of blue and white were requested for the ceremony and for her bouquet. The entire crew and band were coming. Everyone was sworn to secrecy. No one must know about what was going on, or they would be mobbed by adoring fans. After the church ceremony, the wedding party would come back to the Hilton to a suite that they had procured for the reception. The reception was to have a wedding cake, two cases of Dom Perignon champagne, and hors d'oeuvres for about 40-50 people. A full bar was to be provided with a bartender. I was told, just do it, and give him a bill. I scribbled as fast as I could and was told to check with him around lunch time to report that all was handled. The time now was about 2:30 AM, and I had been at work since about 7:00 am the day before. The wedding was to take place about 2:00 in the afternoon on this very day, Monday, November 28th. The 28th of November was a scheduled day off for the tour, and on November 29th, the group would be on their way to another city for another show.

As I finished taking my notes and went to uncurl myself from the floor, I felt a tap tap tap on my shoulder. As I twisted around, there sat the gorgeous Greg Lake. As I tried to keep my mouth from falling open, he asked, do you have time for me now? And would I like a drink? I thanked him but told him I had to get home because my babysitter was waiting, and I needed to redo my notes for the next day. I had a lot to do. Greg said that I looked I could use one drink and truth be known, I needed to sit for a minute to digest what I was being asked to produce in a matter of a few hours. His bodyguard moved one seat over and there I was, having a drink with Greg Lake. Greg had read my brochure and was interested in the concept of the business. He also asked me what was to happen with the wedding.

The crew was already a buzz with their day off and the special wedding that was going to happen on the road. As we chatted, I noticed that time was slipping away. He was easy to talk to and was just a regular guy. Not to mention, he was extremely handsome with that winning smile. I literally had to drag myself away, begging lack of sleep, and I knew that I was only going to get a couple of hours of sleep before the children got up for breakfast. Greg was very polite, stating that he could not walk me to my car, but he would send his bodyguard out with me.

I must have had a look of surprise on my face as he said, "You're new to all this. Let me show you what I am talking about."

Greg, me, and the bodyguard got into the elevator, pushing the ground floor to exit the hotel. As the door opened on the bottom floor, there stood a gaggle of gorgeous women that recognized Greg right away and came screaming to the elevator door as his bodyguard had already pushed the close button. All of us were laughing at the chaos we were witnessing at 2:30 in the morning. The elevator went back to deposit Greg on his floor. The bodyguard and I proceeded to go back down to the lobby of the hotel and on out to my car.

On my hour drive back to my house, I had time to think about my plan of attack to produce this wedding. I collapsed into my bed for a two-hour nap. As I look back, I was way too optimistic. Thank goodness I did not know it at the time!

My first call, as I got my daughter to kindergarten and my son to day care, was to call the bakery at the grocery store where I shopped to order the wedding cake. The baker said I had just made the call-in time for her to put it together. I had no idea that wedding cakes took more doing than just any cake, my first initiation into the wedding world. She promised me she would have the wedding cake that I wanted.

My next telephone call was to the church. I belonged then, and still do, to the First Presbyterian Church of St. Petersburg. The church was the perfect location as it was near the hotel, plus it had this magnificent huge church pipe organ. I reached the minister just before he was leaving to make hospital rounds for the day. He was not real excited about having a ceremony there that afternoon. He asked, "couldn't it be tomorrow?" I told him no. The minister also was not thrilled about having a stranger playing the church organ. As I explained the situation in detail to the minister, he consented to allowing the wedding ceremony to take place and for Keith to play the organ. The fee for the church and the organ was to be paid, no problem. The wedding was to take place at 2 in the afternoon, so the minister would hurry with his hospital rounds.

My next call was to our family florist. Her husband told me she was taking her morning nap, so I had him wake her up. She was not too thrilled to be hearing from me. I told her I needed a bridal bouquet, flowers for the bride's hair, boutonniere, flowers in the church, plus a cake topper and fresh flowers for the buffet and cake tables. She promised me she would have the blue and white flowers at the church at 1:30pm.

At this point, I felt like I was home free. All I needed to do was to call the chef at the hotel and put my order in. It took several minutes for the kitchen to locate the chef and get him on the telephone. I was shocked when he refused to provide the hors d'oeuvres, bar, or bartender for this private party. He told me it was too small of a party for him to be bothered, even after I told him money was no object. I also told him he could fix anything appropriate in the food line to make it easy on himself. He proceeded to tell me I could do the food, liquor, and provide the bartender. He would waive any fees that would normally be charged for me to do the catering. He then told me he was going home; he had had a stressful weekend. The bottom line was that the chef just did not want to be bothered with providing anything for this special occasion.

Oh my god, I was mortified. My great schedule had just gone to pot! I truly had a panic attack. My fingers could not dial fast enough on the phone. I first called my grocery store where I had ordered the wedding cake. The deli departments back then were not as they are now. You just did not have the wide selection of choice like you have today. As time was my big enemy, the deli said they had time to help me out but could not provide everything that I had just dreamed up. I ordered what the deli would do for me and knew that I was going to have to get to the store myself before going to the suite at the hotel.

My next call was to the liquor store that had been helping me provide all the beer and liquor that had been on my contracts. I was hysterical at this point, especially when the store manager told me he would need to call all over town to find two cases of Dom. Again, it was not as readily available then as it is now. I was totally stroking out. I asked him to put together a bar for me for about 40 people, and I would be there about 12:30 to pick it up. And no was the answer to my next question, he did not know of anybody that could bartend at this last minute. I knew my brother in law, Don, was in between classes at college, if I could find him. After the first ring on his apartment phone and he picked up, I just about fainted. Yes, he would start toward the liquor store to pick my alcohol up and get to the hotel to get set up as fast as he could. I called the liquor store back. The manager had located all the Dom Perignon and had an employee running around town picking it all up. He would have his employee deliver the champagne to the hotel. He would have the liquor and mixers ready for my brother in law to pick up within the hour. Now, I just had to get dressed, get to the grocery store, buy some hors d'oeuvres items, pick up the cake, pick up my items from the deli, get to the church, and get to the hotel suite so that I could make the rest of the hors d'oeuvres, not to mention setting up the wedding cake and decorating the food tables.

I did not forget about my children. My darling friend that had baby sat for me the night before was picking the children up from daycare and school. Race, race, race!

As I ran into the church, the flowers were sitting in the back pew. The altar flowers were already in place. Keith was practicing on the organ with the minister sitting in front of the church. I was so happy to see such a serene scene. The music was just beautiful. As the crew, bride and groom arrived, all were disappointed that I could not stay for the service. I was disappointed also, but I really had to hustle to get the suite ready for them. I grabbed the flowers for the hotel and took off. Good grief, I still had hors d'oeuvres to make!

When I got to the hotel, I located a wheeled cart and proceeded to the appointed suite where the reception was to take place. My dear brother in law was there, setting up the bar as I came running in. The hotel chef had a table clothed and skirted for me for the food. I unloaded the cart and started to work. In the kitchen, I put together a cheese and cracker tray, fruit tray, and vegetable tray with dip. I put nuts and mints to the side of the wedding cake as I added some greenery and cut flowers. The deli at the grocery store had made some finger sandwiches and pineapples donned with olives and pickles. I was putting greenery and fresh cut flowers on the buffet table as the crew and the new bride and groom came into the room. By the hair of my chinny chin chin, I had just produced my first wedding reception. Little did I know that years later, I would be a well-known wedding and event planner. For my first wedding, I had about 12 hours' notice. If it had not been for my friends and community connections, I could not have pulled this one off. I also did not know that weddings on the road were not a normal occurrence for a tour, but I had pulled it off. By putting this special wedding together for Bobby and Suzanne, I further put my company on the map in the world of rock n roll. This wedding was to have many spin-offs to my career.

The bride and groom, Suzanne and Bobby, along with Greg Lake, Keith Emerson and Carl Palmer after their wedding ceremony at First Presbyterian Church

Bobby and Suzanne are still married today and have three grown children. I have talked to Suzanne on the phone throughout the years but have not seen her since. The first time I saw Bobby after the wedding, a couple of years had passed. Out of his briefcase came a picture of the total wedding party in front of the First Presbyterian Church that he had been carrying around waiting to give to me. I treasure this picture to this day. Bobby also moved on to other shows in his career. Boomer, as he is called, has been production manager for Bruce Springsteen and Billy Joel. This music business is a crazy, wild business with crews moving back and forth all the time. I have always loved seeing Boomer throughout the years. I have taken his crews cookies. He has treated me to front row seats at many Springsteen and Joel concerts. We have had the opportunity to visit, show pictures of our children growing up, and even meet each other's children. Bobby and Suzanne will always be special friends in my heart.

The ever handsome Greg Lake at the wedding reception

Boomer now works exclusively for Billy Joel. Two of his sons travel with him and his gigantic crew. I just love seeing these grown children who ask me questions about their parents' wedding day so many years ago.

Producing this special occasion for the ELP gang opened more doors for me. The pro-

Don Trubey, our affable bartender for the afternoon

moter of this show heard what I had done; this cemented our business relationship. The Bayfront Center management had heard the positive feedback, and this spurred them to recommend me to other promoters and shows. People in the music touring business were talking about this woman in Florida and her Personal Touch business.

Wedding reception hors d'oeuvres table that I had two hours of total prep time and set up to put together

The ELP gang called me to come to Atlanta to the Omni show on March 6, 1978. I was told that they had some future plans where my services might be needed, so come to Atlanta so we could have some discussions.

I flew to Atlanta the morning of the 6th. It was really great to see everyone. I was extremely curious as to why I was there, and I did not have to wait long. The ELP tour was ending, and plans for the future were going full speed ahead. First, Carl wanted me to arrange a vacation for him at Disney World. There would be three people in his group. He did not want anyone to know who he was. He wanted restaurant menus in his room from area restaurants. Keith had decided to also go to Orlando with his family, and I was to set that up. The biggest and best news was saved for last. The crew and band would be in the Bahamas recording their album Love Beach starting in June. Due to the limited shopping that was available in the Bahamas at that time, would I be willing to take orders for items that they requested from the States and fly those items down to the Bahamas for them? The phone call would come from their assistant in the Bahamas. I was to go shopping for the items that they wanted, then get on a plane to bring those items down to them in the Bahamas. I could not think of a reason not to accept this position. I was excited beyond belief! We shook hands to seal the deal. I was told they would be in touch with further instructions as June got closer. In the meantime, I was to go and enjoy the show. The concert was the same one that had been played in St. Petersburg. It was great to see the entire show from start to finish. I called a cab for myself and went to the hotel to my nice snuggly bed.

The first phone call that I got from the Bahamas came in June 1978 from the band's secretary and organizer in the Bahamas. I just loved this lovely lady from the first moment we talked on the phone.

Midge Trubey

41

She gave me a list of items the band wanted. These could not be found in Nassau to purchase. I remember that running shoes for beach work outs and sake sets were on the list. She laughed when she told me the band wanted me to bring some of that great smoked fish spread that I had gotten for them in St. Petersburg at the famous Ted Peter's. That was another item that served at the wedding reception.

Ted Peter's is a local restaurant and fish smoke house in St. Pete that I have been going to since I was a child. My parents used to take me there when I was little. The owners make a smoked fish spread that is just killer. I loved providing food items that I knew groups could not get anywhere else in the country. The smoked fish spread was just such an item.

I was instructed to go buy some of the spread and fly it to the Bahamas. That was not such a big challenge. I would go buy the smoked fish spread, put it in a cooler, and pack it with dry ice. After I sealed the cooler with silver electrical tape, I was sure it would survive the plane trip down, no problem. Today, I doubt that I could even get it on the plane! The biggest challenge was the next request. Greg wanted to give his manager a Great Dane Harlequin puppy. They found the puppy at a farm in the middle of Florida. Would I drive over, pick the puppy up, and get him to the Bahamas? The question was whether to ship the dog via air or bring the dog as part of my luggage. First of all, the dog cost $600, which was a huge price tag to me in those days. As I checked with the airlines, if I shipped the dog via air, the poor little thing would have to sit on the runway in Miami for two hours to change planes to the Bahamas. If the dog went with me as part of my luggage, the dog would be transferred the same as my bags and there would be no long waiting period between flights in Miami. As it was summer, having a young puppy sit on the tarmac in Miami was just not a good plan. It was decided that I would go on a little road trip to pick the dog up, have the puppy stay with me for a couple of days to settle in, then get on a plane with him and fly to the Bahamas along with the sneakers, sake sets, and smoked fish spread.

My children thought this was the most fun side trip. We drove over, all three of us, to pick up the puppy. "Puppy" is the key here; he was

Sweet Strawberry before the flight to The Bahamas taken in my back yard

huge even as a puppy. That was the sweetest dog. I was scared something would happen to him; he was an expensive item. That "puppy" slept with me for two nights and followed me everywhere. My neighbors quickly heard the story of the puppy, and everyone came over to see him. The children were thrilled and so sorry to see him leave.

Around June 10th, I flew with all my items and the puppy to the Bahamas. I packed the smoked fish spread on dry ice with silver tape around the cooler. I watched the dog being lifted onto the plane in Miami, only a 30-minute change. I was looking for the cooler of fish spread; all the other items were packed in luggage. When I arrived in The Bahamas, I had to go through customs with the dog, suitcases, and cooler of smoked fish spread. The men at customs just shook their heads when I told them about the smoked fish spread. They made me open the cooler and sent me on my way. I met the band's coordinator outside of customs, and off we went to the apartment compound where the crew was staying. The dog immediately went to Greg's house along with the other items he ordered. The other flown items were divided and taken to the Keith and Carl's respective houses.

The ELP coordinator was a great hostess, and we became great friends. We went shopping in the straw market where she bought souvenirs for my children. It had been decided that I was not to pay for anything while I was there -- not even my babysitter back in St. Petersburg. Even my parking at the airport was being paid.

As she and I shopped, we talked and talked. She is the first person that ever called me an "entrepreneur." Good grief, I did not even know what that was. She really bolstered my self image. I realized that I was doing something that no one else was doing. I was very selective when it came to picking out items for my clients, even down to the cantaloupe at the market. I truly had not thought of myself in that context before my friendship with this lovely person.

A couple of months later, I was called a second time to bring more items down to the Bahamas. The smoked fish spread was on the list again. Greg had flown back to the States, but the puppy was still there. He had fallen in love with the dog and had not given him to his manager. The puppy had been named Strawberry. I asked to see Strawberry, and to my surprise, that puppy remembered me, jumping all over and licking me! Big slobbery kisses! Once again, the ELP coordinator, Cheryl, was my hostess. We went shopping and running around Nassau. Again, she paid for the gifts for my children, my babysitter's fee, and airport parking. I did receive a fee for my time spent shopping, plus a fee for my travel time on top of the plane fare.

Midge Trubey

Just before Christmas of that same year, I received a third phone call. The households of all the men were having a terrible time finding Christmas decorations for their houses. It had been decided that Christmas would be celebrated in the Bahamas that year so that they could finish the album. They needed decorations for their Christmas trees and Christmas presents for special people. The list was crazy. Packing it all to take on the plane was a nightmare. Of course, the smoked fish spread was on the list. When I went through customs for the third time carrying my cooler, the customs officials literally laughed that the crazy American woman was here again. They recognized me and just waved me through, not even bothering to open the cooler.

To my surprise, I was told that Greg wanted to see me at his house. I was directed to go straight to his house with all the items I purchased back in the States. I was met at the gates of his house by his bodyguard, the same man I had met at the Bayfront Center the year before. It was hard to believe that over one year had passed since I had met this band. The entire household was decorating for Christmas, and Greg was taking orders from his wife. His daughter was running around with Strawberry. Of course, Strawberry jumped all over me! Strawberry had gotten so big that it was all I could do to keep from falling down when she landed on me.

The Christmas decorations that I had gotten for Greg's house were turned over to his wife. Greg said it was time for him to take a break, and he showed me around the property. A sound studio had been built at the back of the house. The view of the ocean was spectacular. He was on a hill overlooking all that gorgeous Bahamian water. We went back into the house to visit with a glass of sherry. Greg was sitting on the other side of the room as we began talking. The big question was if I enjoyed spending his money this past year. I told him that I thought he had great taste and yes, I had enjoyed the opportunities to come to the Bahamas. I told him how much I enjoyed the hospitality shown to me on all the trips. As we talked, my dear Strawberry came to my side. As I sat down, Strawberry put her head on my shoulder, looking across the room at Greg. The next thing I knew, Greg was grabbing at a pile of cocktail napkins by his chair and came flying across the room. With a handful of cocktail napkins, he grabbed my left breast. I was so startled, I let out a yelp, and the entire household came running. What Greg had seen, and I had not, was Strawberry drooling all over me and down my dress! Greg was trying to stop the drool. I had the biggest drool down my shoulder, down my breast, almost to my waist. The entire house was hysterical. We laughed and laughed. The bad thing was that I was returning to Florida that same day and had no change of clothes. I flew back to Florida with dried dog drool down the left-hand side of my dress, shoulder to waist.

I was personally very disappointed that the album Love Beach did not become a big hit on the record charts. I actually felt like I had had a part in that album. ELP went their separate ways shortly thereafter to pursue individual interests. Again, their music and the great memories that I have from this fantastic group will remain with me always.

The forever dear man, Bobby "Boomer" Thrasher and me, current picture from backstage at Billy Joel

2016 just held terrible news about my friends. Keith Emerson committed suicide in March. I called my friend, Bob. Shock and sadness were shared. Then, in December, Greg Lake died due to cancer. My thoughts and prayers immediately went to his wife and daughter whom I had met so many years ago. ELP would be no more. Time marches on. Boomer (Bob) and I reminisced about the good 'ol days once more. I am still hoping to see Carl on tour sometime in the near future.

These first four contracts opened up the entire field of music entertainment to me. My experiences proved to me that one thing leads to another; I was onto something with my business idea. Not only cooking for concerts, but weddings and party planning. I was more determined than ever to see where this road would take me. I had experienced events and met some wonderfully talented people in the short time that I had been in business. My curiosity was definitely up, and the excitement of creating something from nothing really intrigued me. Plus, I had proven to myself that I could make money for my family.

Sandy's Best Ever Quiche

I have used this recipe forever; everyone has always loved it.

— Serves 4-6 —

✕✕

½ c mayo, not Miracle Whip, not lite mayo, Hellman's is the best

2 tbsp flour

2 eggs, beaten

½ c milk

Mix all the above in your mixing bowl by hand, then add:

½ lb grated Swiss cheese (I have used cheddar and various blended grated cheeses)

1/3 c thinly sliced onion

Optional: add 1 c of fresh vegetables in small pieces

1 c shrimp, or
1 c ham, or 1 c crab

✕✕

Pour this mixture in to a 9" frozen pie crust or unroll a can of Pillsbury croissant dinner rolls. Place the dinner rolls in a 9" pie pan, making your crust, trim the edges. Bake at 350° for 40-45 minutes. Let sit for ½ hour before slicing.

Ken's Pasta Fagioli

Ken makes this for a crowd when he has his Friday night parties "On the deck" in Connecticut.

— Serves 8 - 10 —

3 tbsp olive oil

1 large onion, diced

1 lb Italian bulk sausage

2 cloves garlic, minced

1 - 29 oz. can tomato sauce

5 ½ c of V-8 juice

1 tbsp dried parsley separate on the side

1 ½ tsp dried basil

1 ½ tsp dried oregano

1 tsp salt

1 15 oz can cannellini beans

1 15 oz can navy beans

¼ c Parmesan cheese

1 lb little elbow pasta noodles, cooked al dente, keep

In a large stock pot, brown the first four ingredients and drain off any excess oil.

Add the remaining ingredients with the exception of the noodles. Stir occasionally while heating up on a low burner setting so that nothing sticks to the bottom of your pot. When all hot, add your al dente noodles to your soup, continue to stir occasionally until entire soup is nice and hot.

Serve when all is heated with a side of more parmesan cheese for extra sprinkling.

Midge Trubey

Life on the Road

After my first few shows, I was asked to travel throughout the state of Florida. Holy cow, I was traveling, and I had never imagined that! None of the concert venues in Florida had a kitchen. I always had to make my own kitchen in every building. As long as I had running water and power, I was able to cook.

In every city, I would go to the grocery store, purchase groceries, and come back to the venue to cook like crazy for the remainder of the day and into the night. I got to be friends with almost every major Florida grocery store. After a few months of cultivating relationships with the store managers, I was allowed to write checks for my purchases versus always having to carry so much cash. This might not seem like a big deal today, but back in 1977, there were no ATMs, no check cards, and grocery stores did not take credit cards. I had a check cashing card at every grocery store in Jacksonville, Lakeland, Orlando, St. Petersburg, Tampa, Ft. Myers, Hollywood, Daytona Beach, Miami, Miami Beach, Pensacola Beach, Ft. Walton Beach, and Tallahassee. Each grocery store needed to be a large, full line store. Superstores as Walmart and Sam's Clubs did not exist at this time either. Publix, Kroger, Piggly Wiggly, Winn Dixie, Skaggs, and Albertsons were the stores I looked for. I quickly realized that with cooking for a tour and traveling outside of my hometown area, I needed to develop a better way of producing food. During initial time for me, 1977, the shows traveled with about 30 people needing to eat at each meal. Years later, the shows were so much larger, up to 75-100 people per meal.

I was fortunate that a local St. Petersburg company had one of the best road case building companies in the United States. For those of you that do not know about road cases, let me explain. These are heavy duty boxes built on casters that house everything needed to produce a road show. The cases are built to house guitars, other musical instruments, electrical equipment, sound equipment, and clothing. I went over to their warehouse seeking help making a better traveling kitchen for myself.

My research on developing a kitchen had begun shortly after I started traveling the entire state of Florida cooking for the entertainers and crews. I found out that I was in the company of just two other individuals that traveled with entertainers on a national level. Willie Nelson had his own caterer. This caterer had taken an older crew bus and changed it into a traveling kitchen. The bus was parked outside the concert hall, and the men had to come eat in shifts inside the bus. This idea did not appeal to me for three reasons: the expense of a bus, the crews had to eat in shifts, and I would not be located in the back stage area to keep up with the work schedules of the crews and demands of the bands. The other road cook traveled with the Grateful Dead. This caterer traveled with portable propane gas which scared me to death. I could see myself blowing someone up in a back room or having problems locating propane on the road. Also, propane was not allowed to go through some of the tunnels on the highways. Neither of these cooking systems seemed right for me. I wanted to cook on the road my way; I wanted to be near my guys. I wanted everyone to eat together whenever possible, and I did not want to miss any news about show problems or schedule changes. Any problems with production could affect the feeding schedules. The Personal Touch had only been in business for about a year at this time, but I was already getting the nibble to go on the road nationally.

The local road case company was wonderful in helping me design my "kitchen on wheels". I purchased a full-sized electric range, and they built a road case for it. The case fit down over the entire stove, and naturally the case was on wheels. I had their electrician put a 100' pig tail on the stove so that it could be hotwired anywhere in any facility. High power for any of these shows was never a problem. My electrical problems stemmed from coffee pots and toasters blowing fuses as this everyday type of power was not supposed to be used in these buildings. The stove could roll wherever each building felt comfortable having a cooking area. In some buildings, I cooked on fire escapes, loading docks, walkways into the concert hall. At any location, I could make a kitchen. At the end of the night, the stove would be disconnected, and the top of the road case would be attached. I then bought a full-sized refrigerator whereby the front and back of the road case came off. This meant I could have a refrigerator wherever I was. Hurrah! A normal plug was all that was needed. Finally, I did not need mountains of ice and tubs for my food to stay at the proper temperature throughout the day. Searching for the food I needed under mountains of ice in a large tub was extremely time consuming. The refrigerator could roll wherever I was positioned for my kitchen for that particular day. Having a full-sized refrigerator was wonderful. When I came back from my daily trip to the grocery store, I had a place to put my refrigerated items. When it came time to use an item, it was very easy: open the refrigerator and pull it out. Think about how much we take for granted when it comes to our refrigerators!

Both pictures, Midge working and cooking back stage Courtesy of South Bend Tribune, South Bend, Indiana

I still needed large containers for all the juices, water, milk, and beer that were required for each show. These containers were big, new, plastic trash cans that would hold the volume of liquids needed for each show. Large amounts of ice were needed for the beverages, but each building usually had ice machines for their own concession stands. Arrangements were always made for me to be able to use their ice machines. I then had the case company design a pots and pans case for me. Up until this point, trying to find boxes that would carry all the utensils, pots, and pans needed for each of these shows was truly a hassle. I did not look very professional coming into the concert hall with my equipment in banana boxes. The case I had designed for me was large enough for all the cooking utensils, baking dishes, silverware, pots, and pans. I am a tall woman, so the case was extremely deep and very large. I miscalculated the depth when the height of the wheels was added. I spent the next 15 years being just about the only one on my crew that could stand on her tip toes and reach into the back of this case! I was extremely limber during my days on the road. My little cousin would get a chair and actually climb into the case to get whatever she needed when I was not around. My cousin, Kathleen, was just a jewel on these long road shows. When my cases were built, I was finally prepared to cook for my bands and crews anytime, anywhere. I could actually cook for my clients and truly have a kitchen wherever they were playing their concerts. The cases just barely fit into a work van that I had to purchase around this same time. The cases were so large that creative packing was needed. Gone were the days of loading the groceries into my Volkswagen van along with my pots, pans, and utensils nestled into banana boxes. I was a rock n roll roadie. These three cases were drop shipped and air freighted all across the country. My catering kitchen was forklifted up and down into semi-tractor trailers traveling to different cities on a daily basis. The rule of thumb was my cases were the last to be forked up into the semi-tractor trailer from a show each night and the first to come down the next morning with each new city.

Van Halen

On April 22, 1978, Journey was headlining at Curtis Hixon Hall. I had only been in business roughly nine months. Journey was very hot at the time. This concert would be huge and have 3 acts, rather than 2. Years later, I would realize that this concert would change my career.

The opening act was Ronnie Montrose, featuring Sammy Hagar, and the third act was Van Halen, having just released their first album. Van Halen was just starting to make a name for themselves with the remake of The Kinks You Really Got Me and Runnin' with the Devil. The Van Halen that I knew back in the 70s was comprised of Alex Van Halen, drums, Eddie Van Halen, guitar, Michael Anthony, base, and David Lee Roth, lead singer.

Setting up at Curtis Hixon for three acts was difficult. The building had two large dressing rooms to accommodate two bands, not three. Earlier in the day, it was decided where the bands would go once they all hit the building. Journey and Montrose each had a dressing room. When I asked where Van Halen was going, I was told to set up their table in the men's bathroom in the backstage area. When I went into the bathroom to get their backstage food and beverages set up, I had one immediate question. Where was the eight-foot table to be placed for their rider requests? And no, the M&Ms request was not included at this point and time. There was literally no room for the table. I went to the promoter who informed me that I had to put the table in that bathroom, across the front of the men's urinals - period.

I decided that it was just too gross to set up food and drinks blocking the urinals for a bunch of men. I made all the trays for the dressing room and iced down all the beer, water, and drinks for the band, keeping all the items together back in the kitchen area. I wait-

Midge Trubey

51

ed for the band to arrive. Very close to show time, Van Halen came rushing into the hall. I ran after them, following them into their tiny dressing room/bathroom. The band immediately started complaining, "just great, no food, no drinks, so typical." They turned to find me standing there, and I introduced myself. I told them that I had everything ready for them, but I would not put the table in front of the urinals unless they okayed it. I told them the table could go in the hallway outside their dressing room if they would place someone in their entourage to guard the table and drinks so that no one outside their group would touch the table. I was talking fast and explaining that I was grossed out putting the table in the bathroom in front of the urinals.

All four men stopped moving and turned at the same time to look at me. All four of them thanked me for my consideration in this situation. They instructed me to set up the table outside in the hallway, and they would place someone from their entourage by the table to guard their stuff. In about five minutes, all was in place for the band. Their person was in place guarding their table. The show began shortly thereafter.

At the end of the evening, the four guys found me and thanked me again for taking good care of them. They had liked the food, the service, and the consideration. This simple act of consideration on my part was to carry me for years in a business relationship with Van Halen, I just did not know it at the time. I was to find out years down the road that they never forgot that I refused to place their food in front of the urinals.

Those of you that were and are big Van Halen fans know that Van Halen's rise to the top after 1978 was almost meteoric. Van Halen became so hot, they sizzled, releasing hit after hit. Songs with the titles Dance the Night Away, Jump, Panama, and Hot for Teacher were huge on the charts. As the band rose, they continued touring almost constantly. Van Halen was the main attraction. They were the big headliners; now they got the big dressing room.

Whenever they came into Florida, the band requested that I be their caterer. I traveled with them around Florida. Jacksonville, Ft. Myers, St. Petersburg, and Tampa are the shows that I remember. As they grew in rock n roll stature, their requests grew also. Yes, the famous "no brown M&Ms" was on the rider. I must tell you that touring a different town every day with the request of "no brown M&Ms" was a big pain in the neck. This is how I handled that one. In the rider at that time, the traveling crew was to be fed a hot breakfast, meaning eggs cooked to order and a breakfast meat, such as bacon, sausage, or ham. The truckers were to have cold breakfast, meaning cereals. This never made sense to me as the truckers had just finished driving all night with all the equipment. These guys came into the building tired and ready to go to bed, and all they could have was cold cereal? No one else but them was around at 7 am, so I would cook them a hot breakfast if they would pick the brown and black M&Ms out of the bags for me. No one of higher authority was around, so the truckers and my crew were on our own. While they picked out the M&Ms, I cooked their eggs to order just like the rest of the crew that would follow later. The truckers took the "bad" M&Ms with them to the hotel as a snack when they went to bed. They had a nice hot breakfast, just like the rest of the traveling crew, and I did not have to waste my time picking out M&Ms. It was a win/win situation. As the years went on, the truckers would walk into the building, knowing I would be there, and see the bags of M&Ms on the table along with bowls for separating. It became an unspoken method of operation. As my Melanie got older, she liked to pick the brown M&Ms out of the packages. She called it her "treat!" I did ask David Lee why such a silly request was on their rider. I was told "because we can." That answer was good enough for me. They were at the top of the charts, and they knew it.

The four Van Halen men would come into the building laughing and joking with each other night after night in those late 70s years. They were happy and making lots of money. Eddie, Alex, Michael, and David still shared a dressing room in these early days. It was one big party when they hit the building. All four of them always greeted me like an old friend. At the same time, the road crew was always shocked that the guys never trashed my dressing rooms after the show. The crew would come running night after night, shaking their heads in disbelief that the band put their garbage in the cans, food that was uneaten was left in place on the tables, drinks that had not been drank were in the ice cans left over for the crew. I was told night after night that I was the only caterer in the country that the band did not trash their dressing room. The reason why I was the lucky one all went back to that initial night of our meeting at Curtis Hixon when I would not put their food over the urinals. All the Van Halen men would always thank me for my work. I felt like we were friends, even for just a week of travel about twice a year.

One night in Ft. Myers, the promoter for Van Halen called me into his backstage office. He had special ordered a huge cake in the shape of a guitar with happy birthday wishes written on it for Eddie's birthday. He told me to take it into their dressing room. The band was already in the building with a huge entourage that night. I really did not want to go into the dressing room with this huge cake. In the back of my mind, I was haunted by the fact that I might find this cake later that night all over the place. As I was walking to the dressing room with this gigantic cake, I came up with a plan. As I got to their dressing room door, I got down on my knees holding the cake in my outstretched arms. I juggled the cake as I knocked loudly on their door. It was the time of night just before show time when you did not go into the dressing room at all, so a loud knock was not the norm. The door flew open with David Lee and Eddie first, and Michael was close behind. The look on their faces when they saw me on my knees with this huge cake was priceless. As they looked down at me, jaws open, I began my talk. I told them that this cake was a gift from the promoter for Eddie's birthday. The cake was to be eaten, not to be put on the floor, ceiling, or mirrors of the dressing room. I began to inch my way, still on my knees, into their dressing room begging them to have mercy on me. I did not want to clean up cake at the end of a long day. The guys were hysterical with laughter. David begged me to get up off my knees as someone could be watching with a camera, and it would not look good to see a woman on her knees coming into the dressing room juggling this big guitar birthday cake. As laughter was prevailing, I reiterated that I would not get off my knees until I had a solemn promise from all four of them that they would behave themselves with this birthday cake. They promised, so I got off my knees, and we all sang Happy Birthday to Eddie. I had made a total fool out of myself in front of the guys and their guests, but I got my message across: no messy cake at the end of the night.

As the story spread about the birthday cake that night, the crew began taunting me that cake would be everywhere. They said the band could not and would not resist having fun with the cake. When the band left the building that night, all of us, me at the end of the line, went running into the dressing room to survey the expected damage. I am proud to tell you that the cake was totally untouched. The Happy Birthday Eddie Guitar Cake was still sitting on the table where I had placed it. The crew was in disbelief. I think I even made money that night betting a few folks $5.00 that my Van Halen guys would not trash my dressing room that night. I was one happy woman!

As the early 80s continued, Van Halen just got hotter on the charts. With that growth came a change in the band. Eddie got married. I never officially met Valerie Bertinelli; I just adored her on television like thousands of other fans. I just caught her running to and from the dressing room on a couple of occasions, and primarily I saw her from the back side. Also, as the guys used to be in one big dressing room together, all laughing and holding court together, that changed. Each man now wanted his own dressing room with his own personal set up. As I look back on this new arrangement, the laughter between the four of them off stage had ceased. Michael was always laughing, kind, and easy to talk to. Eddie was more withdrawn and really wanted his privacy. Alex requested that his dressing room be set up for mediation, yoga mats and all, and leave-me-alone attitude. David's dressing room was set up with a gym for working out.

David Lee and Eddie Van Halen both loved attention onstage. David pranced, sang, and jumped. Eddie was known for his fabulous guitar work. I always thought Eddie was known for his beautiful smile and dancing eyes. When Eddie was smiling, you had to smile back. His entire face would light up like a light bulb. Clouds were forming in his personal life as well as conflict between him and David Lee. On tour, the men stayed separated, doing their shows and raking in the money.

One of the last times I worked with Van Halen was around 1984. Jump was their big hit; backstage we would sing "Hump" just for fun. The tour was ending in Jacksonville. I had been with Van Halen, as usual, from the time they had entered Florida approximately five days before this Jacksonville date. The band wanted to have an end-of-the-tour party for the crew and their guests. I want to remind you once again, there were no cell phones at this time nor computers. As the day of the party progressed, the band called with orders for what they wanted to have that night. First of all, the party was to start about 1:00 AM after the show. By starting the party then, all the trucks could be packed, showers taken, and the men would be ready to party. Also, I said "men" because during this time frame, very few women were on the crews, not like today. This party in Jacksonville was to be a doozie.

About midafternoon, they ordered a balloon drop for the end of the encore song. What a scramble that was to find enough balloons to go up to the ceiling of the Coliseum on such short notice. The balloons were installed about one hour before the show started. The promoter found a local band to start playing at 1:00 am. The backstage area was to be transformed into a garden-type setting while the band played onstage during their show. The backstage area was to be carpeted with green indoor/outdoor carpeting. Street lanterns were rented to provide lighting for a park-like setting. Palm trees were brought in. Pinball machines were brought in for a game room off to the side. Food was ordered (thank God) from local restaurants:

Chinese and barbeque. I was coordinating the placement of all the items as they were coming in along with my regular tour responsibilities. Round tables and chairs were set up in front of a specially-built stage in the backstage area for the hired band to play during the party. Tablecloths were placed on the guest tables. Two bars were set up with full alcohol, and two bartenders were hired to serve the guests. All this set up was accomplished while Van Halen was finishing their set and the crew was breaking down the concert. It was a hustle, trust me. What I remember most about the party was the graciousness of the Van Halen band.

About midway through the party, the four men took to the stage. A tour story was told about each man as each one was called up on the stage. The stories were funny; sometimes stories were told that no one thought the band was aware of what had happened, or that particular crew guy had a secret nickname that no one knew the band was aware of. There was so much laughing. It impressed me that the band took the time to acknowledge each and every crew member. Each person was given an envelope with extra money. Many tours don't end with gratuities. Often, the stars don't even know the names of those that support them backstage. This is why this rare end-of-tour party was so special. I will always remember Van Halen, the four original men, Eddie, Alex, Michael, and David Lee as a class act. I bet you're surprised. These men were a hoot to travel with around the state of Florida, and these are stories I will always remember.

Crustless Spinach & Cheese Quiche

I have been making this way before I had my business. My father in law, Les Trubey, was a vegetarian.

— Serves 4-6 —

◇◇◇

3 - 10 oz packages of frozen spinach

3 jars of Old English cheese

24 oz of cottage cheese

9 eggs, beaten by hand

9 tbsp of flour

◇◇◇

Let spinach thaw at room temperature. Put in your colander, run hot water over spinach until there are not more frozen crystals. Take your hands and squeeze all the water out of the spinach. Set aside. Mix together the Old English cheese, the beaten eggs and flour. Add the squeezed spinach, breaking apart as you add. Add the cottage cheese. Blend well. Place in a buttered 9-13 dish. Bake at 350° for 45 minutes or until the middle is set. The top should be a golden color. Let sit before you cut into squares and serve. You should get about 12 nice sized squares.

Midge Trubey

Quick Beef Stroganoff

You will notice that quick is the big plus in recipes for me when I was on the road, the clock was always ticking, time was always short.

– Serves 6 –

3 lbs of filet mignon, cut into ¼-inch strips

3 tbsp of margarine

1 large sized onion, sliced thinly

3 cloves garlic, minced or granulated garlic can be used to taste (not everyone loves garlic the way I do)

3 - 10 ½ oz cans of condensed cream of mushroom soup, (I always used Campbell's soup)

3 c of sour cream, I think Daisy is the best

12 oz of sliced bottled mushrooms, undrained, or use 2 pt of fresh mushrooms, washed and sliced

6 tbsp of ketchup

6 tsp Worcestershire sauce

2 bags wide egg noodles

Cook noodles as package directs, drain well. Add two tablespoons of butter and two teaspoons of poppy seeds (can be eliminated). Toss together.

Melt your shortening in your skillet adding onion, garlic and mushrooms. Cook until onion is soft, do not overcook as you now need to add your beef. Watch carefully as to just brown your tenderloin, do not overcook, just brown, so that your meat will be nice and tender. In your mixing bowl, mix you cream of mushroom soup, sour cream, catsup and Worcestershire sauce. Add this to your meat. Stir to blend completely with your meat. Heat through, do not boil. Serve immediately over your noodles.

If I had vegetarians in the group, I would keep the noodles and stroganoff separate for serving. If you are fixing at home, serve your stroganoff over your noodles. If you have left over noodles, there are a million things you can do.

The Show Must Go On!

As I've said before, my backstage schedule for most tour shows is set in stone. Breakfast is at 6 am, and lunch at 11 am. I set up the dressing rooms at 4 pm, have dinner ready at 6 pm, then restock and straighten up the dressing rooms at show time. Once the show gets started, I had to get beverages up on stage, prepare after-show food, then clean up and move on. Somewhere in that schedule, I would also have to shop for food. There are no exceptions to this schedule, period. The show is going on, and you have a job to do, even if the rest of the world may not understand that.

Back in the 80s, I was in Orlando to cater for Arlo Guthrie at the Bob Carr Auditorium. For those of you who didn't live through the 80s, there were no cell phones, no debit cards, and grocery stores did not take credit cards. I was paid in cash at the end of each concert and had designed my own money belt to carry it around. Still, I really didn't feel comfortable carrying large amounts of cash around. When it was time to go on my grocery runs, I was always hoping to pay with a check. At that time, if you wanted to use a check to pay for groceries, you had to qualify for a check-cashing card with that grocery store before your purchase by proving you weren't going to bounce checks. I had check-cashing cards from as many grocery stores as possible around Florida.

A typical day of grocery shopping, Wichita, Kansas

I shopped numerous times at the Publix in Orlando near the Auditorium. When I ran out to pick up a few additional items for the show after lunch, I took my check book to have a talk with the manager to get my check-cashing card. I walked into the store and went directly to the Customer Service area. The manager's office was located just behind the cigarette counter and the bottle return center. I walked up to the cashier at the counter and asked to see the manager. As the manager came out of his office, I walked around the counter, and we shook hands. I proceeded to make my request to get a check-cashing card from his store.

At that moment, a man came around the corner and walked through the employee entrance to get behind the counter. He was dressed in black pants and a white shirt. I thought he was a bag boy, as the guys were called back then, until he announced, "this is a stick up, no one move." I literally thought it was a joke. I was about to laugh when someone started shoving me from behind. I turned to tell this person to quit shoving me only to find another man in a white shirt and black pants. This one was holding a big black gun.

I immediately went into survival mode. The second man shoved the gun in my back. He told me to stand at the counter with the cigarette girl and act like nothing was going on. A third man appeared, dressed the same, and went from register to register telling the cashiers to empty their drawers into his money bag. At the same time, the first man pushed the store manager into his office and demanded that he open up the store's safe.

The poor manager was so nervous, he kept forgetting the combination of the lock. I was still standing next to the cigarette cashier with a gun in my back. I was suddenly very aware of the jewelry I had on and the money belt I had hidden under my clothes. I twisted my rings to hide the diamonds and tugged at my t-shirt, hoping no one would go looking for the thousand bucks I had on me.

Customers were coming up to get deposit money for their glass returnable soda bottles and to buy cigarettes. The cashier and I were scared to death that someone would realize the store was being robbed and all hell breaking loose. As the manager continued to fumble with the locks, the first robber became very agitated. I thought that he was going to shoot the manager, then run out of the office and shoot anyone standing in his way -- which was me.

I had an idea. I began to inch my way to the end of the counter, thinking I could dive for the floor on the other side of the counter to dodge any bullets that I thought might come. As I inched toward the counter opening, a young mother approached the counter with the most darling little baby in her buggy. I was terrified she and the baby would also become hostages. I leaned over the counter to touch her baby, saying what an adorable child she had, and asking if I could hold the baby, all along moving closer to the counter opening. The woman thought I was a crack pot, which is what I wanted her to think. My deterrent worked, and she immediately pushed her baby away from the counter and went further into the store.

The man with the gun noticed my shift to the counter opening and commanded me to freeze. I inched a little more to my diving position, covering the move by saying I was just trying to get out of his angry friend's way. My cover didn't work, and gun man told me to stop moving. I froze. In these few short minutes inching forward, I felt like I had given myself a fighting chance of not getting shot. I felt I could successfully dive to the floor on the other side of the counter and maybe save my life.

I have never been so scared in my life. I thought about my children, not seeing them again, and not seeing them grow up, all because I needed a check-cashing card from the grocery store in Orlando. I was watching the third man cleaning the money out of the registers. The bewildered cashiers were looking toward to the office seeing a strange woman (me) and the cigarette counter girl, just smiling like everything was okay. The shouting in the manager's office was getting louder. Two thoughts came to me in that moment. One, these guys weren't wearing masks. I could clearly identify all of them. And two, that was enough to get me killed.

Out of the corner of my eye, I could see movement outside the glass store front windows. The Orlando police department had pulled up in front of the store like a massive raid. I would find out later that an off-duty policeman had walked in front of the store, looked in, and realized that a robbery was in progress. At least eight police cars came screeching up from all directions, lights flashing, to block the entrance to the store. Chaos erupted.

The man with the gun at my back hollered to his friend in the office that the police were there. As the man ran out of the office, I dove for the floor on the other side of the counter. As I hit the floor, the two men ran out from behind the counter to the back of the store. Seeing them flee, the third robber ran across the front of the store to join his buddies. No shots had been fired.

I picked myself off the floor, chaos and screaming coming from all directions. Then I did something only a tour crew member would understand. I walked out the front doors of the Publix, got into my van, and drove to the Winn Dixie on the other side of the street. I still had a huge list of groceries to buy, and I needed to get back to the auditorium and get dinner started.

I walked into the Winn Dixie, grabbed a cart, and started shopping with my list. Lo and behold, whom should I see but that darling woman with the little baby that I just saved from being a hostage at the Publix bottle counter. I couldn't help myself; I ran to talk to her. I had to explain what had happened, and that I wasn't a crack pot! She noticed me coming and immediately tried to turn to get away from me. She told me to back away saying that she had left the store across the street because I scared her. I babbled my story about the gun in my back and the tears started to fall. I told her I was so glad that she had left the store. This kind woman said that she thought that I was in shock and walked me over to the Winn Dixie manager's office to sit down to compose myself.

I wouldn't leave my grocery cart filled with my items behind, though, and pushed it with us to the manager's office. The gentle manager listened to my story. He had watched the screeching police from his office and knew that something bad was happening across the street. He insisted on calling the Publix, knowing the police would be looking for me. The police department had commandeered the store phone and in seconds, the chief of detectives was on the phone with me. He asked me to return to the store to give them a statement. I told him I was under contract with the City of Orlando for the day, and I had to return to Bob Carr Auditorium, otherwise there would be trouble in the auditorium that night when dinner was not served. He promised me that he just wanted to see me, and then I could proceed on with my day and get back to the auditorium.

I walked back into the Publix through the police security and toward the manager's office. As I approached the all-too familiar office area, the manager, surrounded by police, saw me and immediately pointed saying, "there she is." I gave a brief statement to the detective that I had talked to on the phone. As I was hurrying to get back to work, the detective told me he would come to the Bob Carr Auditorium for a detailed interview after dinner had been served backstage. Just before I hurried out of the Publix, I asked him what had happened to the men that committed the robbery. The man that had held the gun on me had run out the back door of the store into the parking lot waving his gun. He had been shot, not fatally, and taken to the hospital. The other two men had tried to hide in the women's bathroom and had been apprehended when the police were sweeping the store. Suddenly, I knew how lucky I had been.

I hopped back into my van and drove as fast as I could back to the auditorium. When I walked in, my staff was very worried as I had been gone a long time. When I saw them and began to tell them what happened, I finally realized what a dangerous ordeal I had just been through. I began to shake and cry, and my staff took over finishing up the dressing rooms and cooking dinner. As the word spread backstage what had happened to "Mom," the men all came to see me, even Arlo. He was so very nice with his concern, as were the entire crew. After dinner, the police showed up for a detailed interview just before the show started. I was not much good for the rest of the night; everyone took pity on me and let me chill. I watched some of the show out front of the house, which is something I never did. I watched as Arlo told the crowd that this night would be the last night that he would ever sing Alice's Restaurant. He was bored with the song and wanted to also be known for his other music. Throughout the years, I have asked anyone that knows Arlo if he has ever sung the song again. I have been told no, never again. I wonder if he has stuck to his promise?

Midge Trubey

Chicken Chip Bake

This recipe has been used for ladies' luncheons since my Junior League days.

– Serves 6-8 –

◇◇◇

4 c cubed cooked chicken

4 c sliced celery

1 ½ c mayo (Hellman's or Duke)

2/3 c toasted slivered almonds

4 tbsp fresh lemon juice

1 small onion diced very small

1 tsp salt

◇◇◇

Combine all ingredients. Mix well with a large spoon and pile into a greased baking dish. Sprinkle the top with shredded cheddar cheese (can be mild or sharp, whichever you prefer), roughly one cup or a little more (you want the top even with cheese). Then sprinkle the top with about one cup of crushed potato chips. Bake at 425° for 20 minutes or until hot (uncovered). Serve with fresh fruit as a side and/or fluffy white rice.

Rice & Cheese Casserole

Great side dish for chicken or fish.

– Serves 12 –

2 c uncooked long grain rice

2 c shredded sharp cheese

1 c salad green olives with pimentos, drained

2 c chopped tomatoes

1 medium Vidalia onion, chopped

5 tbsp melted butter

2 c water

Salt and pepper to taste

In large mixing bowl, combine all ingredients and pour into 3-quart casserole. Cover and bake at 350° for 1 hour. (Casserole will set up while cooking)

Midge Trubey

Making Friends for Life

I am lucky in that I have many special memories of a lot of people. I call them "interesting, bright spots" of a crazy career. There are times when you totally connect with a client. I believe these special happenings are the icing on your cake of life.

John Denver sang the most beautiful songs. Did you know he liked to play ping pong? Imagine rounding a corner backstage to see him playing ping pong! He was a great player. You can learn a lot of trivia when you travel with people.

Chuck Mangione had his father run all his concessions, selling his t-shirts and tapes. Papa Mangione guarded those t-shirts like they were gold. When you are working for an entertainer, one of the most sought-after concert souvenirs for those working the show is the shirt. The old saying, "I went, and I have the t-shirt to prove it," was always important to all working staff. Papa would not just give the shirts away. His job was to sell, and he took that responsibility seriously. You would ask for a t-shirt, but he would say no with a smile on his face. One year, a runner finally brought me a t-shirt from Papa. I was the one with the smile on my face that night. The t-shirt was red with the silhouette of Chuck and his name in bright yellow.

Ray Charles

The genius, Ray Charles, was one of my most cherished happenings. I worked for him early on in my career. The first show was May 26, 1978, at the Tampa Theatre in Tampa, Florida. Ray Charles had always been one of my favorite artists for several reasons. First, the man could play the piano like no one else, in my book. I had studied piano when I was a child. The fact that he could not see, and he could play the piano with such soul totally brought me under his spell. When you add the great tunes Busted, Georgia On My Mind, Hit the Road Jack, and What'd I Say, well, it just does not get any better than that. His back-up girls were awesome, as was his band. Choirs were often added, and you could not help but be blown away. The total package was a thrill for any concert goer.

The rule backstage was, we were not to approach Mr. Charles to say anything. He was brought into the building and into his dressing room, led to and from the stage, and then he was led out of the venue. I also learned that he had many grandchildren that were the ages of my little children, stuffed into the tiny, backstage area that was Tampa Theatre. As the years of my working continued, I was lucky enough to be asked back again and again to cater for him. Belton Raspberry was his road manager at the time. I asked Belton if I could sit behind Mr. Charles cross-legged on the floor to watch his performance behind the stage curtain. I was thrilled when I was given the OK. As soon as he was led on stage, I would sit directly behind him, on the floor, for the entire show. He would sit at the gigantic grand piano, rocking to and fro, piano bench legs swaying and bending while throwing his legs up in the air, all along never missing a beat or lyric. I was enthralled. I asked Belton if the piano bench had ever cracked, throwing him on the stage floor? I was told, yes, it does happen, and the stagehands would just run to get him up, put another bench under him, and the show would continue. To be able to watch such talent flow through someone's body, head to toe, is still one of my greatest memories. The man was truly a genius.

His grandchildren were just darling. When Mr. Charles was in Tampa, he had a huge family gathering. After my first concert with him, I knew all his grandchildren would be coming to the theatre. The children had literally nowhere to go. The backstage area at Tampa Theatre is almost nonexistent, with very tiny rooms and very tiny hallways. To cater to any group was a challenge at that venue, but for little children, it was a nightmare. I would bake cookies for the children and take coloring books and crayons to keep them from running back and forth in this tiny area backstage. Running backstage was not an option, plus it was not safe. I looked forward to seeing the kids, and they looked forward to their cookies and having something to do while waiting to see their grandfather. The families would come backstage about two hours before show time, then take their seats for the show, then come back after the show to say goodbye. This continued for several years, me working all day, watching Mr. Charles come and go, seeing the children growing up, and sitting behind Mr. Charles during the concerts.

I learned that his travel case held his coffee, gin for his coffee, and his specially-designed eating utensils. His sense of smell was extraordinary. He would walk into his dressing room and immediately ask where the fruit was because he could smell it. He always ate in private; his privacy was well-protected, as was his safety.

One year, I felt comfortable enough to ask Belton if I could meet Mr. Charles. Belton relayed my request to Mr. Charles, and I was given a time after the concert to be at his dressing room door for my introduction. I must say, I was a nervous wreck! When I was ushered into the dressing room by Belton, all I could stumble out of my mouth was what an honor and pleasure it was to finally meet him after so many years, and to tell him how much I loved his music. As I am stumbling all over myself about what a pleasure it was to meet him, he was telling me what a pleasure it was for him to finally meet me! I said to him, oh, no, it was my pleasure to meet him, he said, oh, no, it was a pleasure for him to meet me. We both wound up laughing all the while holding our handshake. Then he explained to me that for years, he had heard how nice I was to the children with the home-baked cookies and the coloring books. He said he had wanted to thank me for my kindness. I was just floored. I believe I loved him more after our meeting than ever before.

I just never thought this world would be without Ray Charles. I had grown up with his music, watched him on television, show after show. I have had the privilege of sitting behind him on stage watching him perform. For me, it was like one day Ray Charles just disappeared from life. But that is life. I don't think we will ever see anyone like him again, at least in my lifetime. When Jamie Foxx portrayed him, which was brilliant, I cried through most of the movie. The genius is gone, but the music of Ray Charles will live on.

Mr. Charles coming into the Tampa Theatre, Tampa, Florida

Eddie Money

I have many stories of my friendship with Eddie Money. Eddie played in St. Petersburg many, many times throughout the years. I have always tried to get to all of them when I have been in town and when my schedule permitted. One particular time, he was playing a concert in the park in downtown St. Petersburg. St. Pete has a gorgeous waterfront park where a lot of concerts are played. That day was truly stunning, the waterfront, the weather, great music, and watching the sun go down. I had been backstage with Eddie's wife watching the show having a great time. Some of his children were with him on this tour, and they were running around backstage playing in the grass. When his set was finished, the sun was long gone. I asked Eddie what he was going to do for dinner; it was definitely after the dinner hour. I knew the children would be hungry as well as he and his wife. He told me that he had no particular plans, so this is what we dreamed up on the spot.

Only a few blocks from where the concert had taken place was my banquet facility, Mansion By the Bay. The Mansion staff was cleaning up from a wedding earlier in the day. I knew that my walk-in refrigerator had food. Eddie and I thought it would be fun to go there, and he and I could cook up dinner in the kitchen together, just like the old days on the road. Even Eddie Money would come visit me in my makeshift kitchen when I was cooking. It was decided that he would sign his autographs, then he, his wife, children, and manager would come over to Mansion for dinner. Now, these were the days of cell phones. I called my Mansion staff and told them what was happening. I asked them to set up tables and chairs for dinner in the sunroom, leave the lights on, and go on home. Well, that was not about to happen! My chefs went nuts when they heard that Eddie Money was coming for dinner. They were not about to let me in the kitchen; they wanted to cook for him. My Mansion manager was not about to leave, because he wanted to stay also. Well, so much for Plan A. The men at the Mansion were taking over, so I was to sit and enjoy my friends while they would take care of everything.

After the autographs were signed a large group of adoring female fans were gathering in the park waiting for Eddie's exit. I led the two vans from the back stage area with my car to the back parking lot of Mansion By The Bay. Naturally, as soon as we pulled out of the park, the girls went running after the vans. The vans were faster than the girls and Eddie's entourage was able to get into the Mansion before the girls caught up. When the girls saw the vans in the parking lot, the girls came around to the front doors of the Mansion to stand around. I had turned the front lights off, which looked like Mansion was closed. I went out front and told the girls that Eddie was not inside, it had been a trick, and asked them to leave. To my shock, they left! Eddie was watching this from the inside windows, laughing.

As we opened up some wine and beers to kick back, I was able to tell him the story about Mansion by The Bay. Drinking a soda, he told me that he had recently gotten out of rehab, and that he was clean and sober. He talked about how he needed to watch his health as he had all these darling children that needed to be raised and had his gorgeous wife, who was sitting there with him. We talked about how the music business can eat you up and spit you out if you allow it. Make no bones about it, it's a hard business.

Eddie had always wanted to meet my longtime boyfriend, who is my husband now. Ray was coming into the back of the kitchen having worked another function. I told Eddie I would go get him so he could join us. Eddie was excited to meet him. On this night, Ray refused to come out of the kitchen. He never thought Eddie was a true friend, therefore always grumbling. On this night, refused to come out of the kitchen. His excuse was that he was not dressed correctly. All of us were in shorts -- it is Florida! I was crushed. As I walked back out to my friends, Eddie took one look at my face and said, "he's not coming out, is he?" I told him no. Eddie could always also read people pretty easily. He then said, "don't tell me Ray is one of those husbands that thinks you were a groupie on the road?" I said, "Eddie, this has been a major problem from day one of our relationship. Ray does not get the difference between a groupie and the work that I did on the road."

My buddy, Eddie, says "take me to the kitchen, and I will take care of this right now." Into the kitchen we went. We then proceeded to the back of the kitchen so that I could introduce Eddie to Ray. Eddie Money is a very easy-going kind of guy. He immediately stuck his hand out for a handshake and proceeded to tell Ray about my cooking on the road and how long we had been friends. Eddie is a charmer, and he did charm Ray. I was in shock. Eddie asked Ray to join us for dinner. He wanted Ray to meet his wife, whereby Ray was Mr. Pleasant and said he would be right out. As Eddie and I walked arm in arm back out to the sunroom, Eddie gave me a squeeze stating, "I think I handled that one!" We grinned and the dinner party got started with Ray joining us.

Eddie was interested in the story of the building itself, Mansion By the Bay. It was built in 1901, and our resident ghost had been seen on several occasions. I only talked about our ghost to a select few, and I was afraid it would scare some people from using the facility for their events and weddings. The ghost was a she, and she liked playing tricks on people at night. We were telling these stories as our dinner was served. The talk was lively, fun, and relaxed.

After dinner, Eddie asked if he could take his boys upstairs to look for the ghost, saying "Midge, don't turn the lights on upstairs." I can still hear Eddie Money chasing his boys around the upstairs of Mansion with the boys squealing, "daddy, quit scaring us!" Eddie was running going "Woo, woo!" The running on the hard wood floors was hysterical in itself as this went on for quite a while. Those of us downstairs had a good laugh; a Dad playing ghost with his boys. This is my most favorite Eddie Money story.

Eddie Money remains a man for whom I will always have a fond affection, not only for his music, but for the man himself. So, to my dear friend, I say "Shake Your Money Maker" in heaven. I will be listening.

Seafood À La Benson

George Benson loved this one. One night he asked me what the name was, therefore, the name. This made him smile his lovely broad grin.

– Serves 10-12 –

◇◇◇

24 oz scallops uncooked, pat dry

12 oz shrimp, peeled, deveined, uncooked, pat dry

24 oz flakey white fish (I use grouper), cut into small bites, pat dry

1 small onion, chopped

4 tbsp butter

1 - 10 ½ oz can of cream o f mushroom soup

1 c whole milk

Dash of pepper and salt

2 c shredded sharp or mild cheese (your preference)

2 frozen packages or frozen French style green beans, blanched, drained and patted dry, still warm

2 c crushed Ritz crackers

4 tbsp of melted butter, for top of casserole

◇◇◇

Cook onion in 4 tablespoons butter till tender, do not brown. On simmer, add soup, milk, pepper and salt, 1 cup of shredded cheese, stir until cheese melts and everything is blended well together. In a separate bowl, mix the green beans with the scallops, shrimp and fish bites together. Grease your baking dish with butter. This is a layered dish. First place your French cut green beans and seafood at the bottom of your casserole dish. Pour your soup mixture evenly over the top of your seafood mixture. Sprinkle the top with the remainder 1 cup of shredded cheese. In a smaller bowl, mix your Ritz crackers and melted butter and sprinkle on the top of your casserole dish. Bake 350° for 30-45 minutes or until casserole is bubbly with crackers browned on top. Serve with white rice or wild rice.

Barbara's Spinach Pie

My sister-in-law gave me this one. Yummy!

◇◇◇

2 lbs of ground hamburger meat (I used 1 lb. ground hamburger and 1 lb. ground lamb)

1 large onion, chopped

1 package frozen chopped spinach, thawed and squeezed dry

1 stick of butter

1 large green pepper chopped

½ c parsley

1 large clove of garlic, chopped

1 c feta cheese, drained

3 large eggs

Salt and pepper to taste

16 sheets of phyllo dough

◇◇◇

Preheat oven to 375° and use a 9x13 baking pan.

In a large skillet over medium heat, brown beef. Add onions, spinach, parsley, garlic and salt and pepper.

Cook stirring mixture until onions are clear, about 3-5 minutes.

Remove from heat. Add green peppers, cheese, eggs and mix well.

Brush your baking pan with some butter. Place one sheet of phyllo dough at a time on the bottom of your pan and up the sides brushing with butter after each sheet is used using only 8 sheets for this bottom layer. Spoon beef mixture evenly over your phyllo dough bottom. Cover with remaining phyllo dough sheets brushing with butter with each layer. Bake for about 40 minutes until top is a golden brown.

We love this with a Greek Salad from our famous Greek Restaurant, Athenian Gardens, and serve a crusty hard roll with butter. This dinner is so yummy and baklava for dessert tops this meal off as one of our family all time favs.

Ray's Secret Fruit Dip

I love this easy dip for great presentation when using fresh strawberries. Dip in the center surrounded by gorgeous big strawberries.

◇◇

**Equal parts of
whipped cream
cheese and
marshmallow fluff.**

◇◇

Let container of whipped cream cheese get room temperature, mix together with an equal amount of jarred marshmallow fluff and refrigerate until close to serving time. At serving, this needs to be to room temperature.

Mudge Trubey

73

The Original Blues Brother, Sam Moore

Let me take you back to 1966, my graduating year from high school and the beginning of my college days. I loved to dance the night away, as the old saying goes. Give me those special sounds, beats, and words, and I would become the dancing fool. Rhythm and blues totally captivated my music world. In high school, there was a club called The Joker Club. My high school friends and I would pile into our cars, drive to the other side of town, and dance all night. When I went to college in the fall of 1966, my dancing days were just beginning. I went to college at the University of Maryland, quickly pledged a sorority, and my party days were on a roll. I also had a college boyfriend who was in a fraternity, so party was the name of the game. Every Friday and Saturday night, you could find us dancing somewhere in the surrounding area of the University. My most favorite songs of the era were Sam and Dave's Hold On, I'm Coming and Soul Man. When those songs were played either on the record player or by a live band, you absolutely could not sit still. Then came the songs I Thank You and When Something Is Wrong with My Baby. Sam and Dave were one of my favorites; I loved their music.

Who would guess that years later, about 1980, I would have the opportunity to meet my "Soul Men" face to face? Sam and Dave were opening for the nostalgia band Sha Na Na on a tour throughout Florida. The Personal Touch Catering was hired by the promoter to make the tour with the bands for the entire state dates. Sha Na Na was a great act at this time and had a huge following. The concert was promoted as a family show. I liked Sha Na Na, but I was absolutely thrilled that Sam and Dave were on the billing.

For me, the contract was pretty basic. Feed the crew breakfast, lunch, and dinner. A dressing room for Lenny, a dressing room for Bowser, a dressing room for the rest of the Sha Na Na guys, and a small dressing room set up for Sam and Dave. The Sha Na Na band was included in the head count for dinner, but the Sam and Dave group was not. I was paid only for those included in the head count numbers, but never for other people that were not pre-approved by the promoter. It was made clear to me that Sam and Dave were not to be included. Ok. This meant that the group was to get their dinner on their own, not at the show. This comes from the original contract that Sam and Dave cut when they joined the tour. Well, as you have learned already, the fact of eating away from the concert hall is not very practical or timely. Sam and Dave's dressing room consisted of some beverages and a deli tray, definitely not dinner food. The first day of the tour, they came running in, starving and pushing the time frame for their opening number. I had finished serving dinner for everyone else, and I had several dinner portions still available. I always made more food than what was called for by the contracts.

Well, here were my very own Hold On, I'm Coming guys standing in front of me, hungry. I ran back to my kitchen area and proceeded to make up some dinner plates to take back to the dressing room. Mind you, I had already fed the number of people that I was required to feed, and this was my left-over food. The promoter saw me walking into the dressing room with this food and verbally jumped all over me in front of Sam and Dave. The argument that ensued was around the fact that the promoter thought I would be billing him for unauthorized meals at the end of the show. I assured him that I would never take it upon myself to charge him for food that he had not pre-approved. I was not going to bill him for the food that I was giving to Sam and Dave, as it was dinner food that had not been consumed under the regular head count figures. This discussion got very heated. Sam and Dave heard it as it was right outside their dressing room. I never liked confrontations, and by the time I got into the dressing room with their dinners, I was a tad rattled. Sam and Dave thanked me for the food but were very apologetic for getting myself into hot water with the promoter. I was more embarrassed for the promoter since I thought his ranting and raving was over the top and out of line. He was not paying for the meals, so why be such a jerk? The Sam and Dave group said that they did not want me getting into trouble. I immediately told them that I would be feeding them the rest of the Florida tour, but I would have to sneak the dinners into their dressing room. I also told them how much I loved their music, and this was my way of thanking them for all the wonderful dancing they had provided for me in my younger days. They seemed really appreciative of my compliments, and off they went to the stage to start the show.

On most of the concerts I worked, I had clearance to go wherever, including on and around the stage. Well, this night was truly a thrill for me. I followed the guys up on stage and proceeded to dance their entire set in my own little world, secluded behind road cases. I was in heaven, dancing by myself to the live music of the original Sam and

Dave. As their set concluded, I ran to check on Sha Na Na to make sure they were all set to go on stage.

The next day of the tour, in a different Florida city, the same daily schedule took place. Breakfast, lunch, dinner, dressing room set ups -- and my sneaking dinner into Sam and Dave's dressing room -- followed by my wild self-party-dancing behind them where no one could see.

By the time we reached St. Petersburg a few days later, my children were dying to see one of their favorites, Sha Na Na. I had my babysitter bring the children down after dinner so that they could meet their idols and see the show. I also introduced them to Sam and Dave. Sam actually took the time to talk with my children, something my children never forgot.

My few days on the road with this tour were amazing for me. I had the opportunity not only to meet one of my most favorite singing groups, but had actually been able to provide food for them and relive my college days by dancing my heart out. The tour continued outside of Florida, and I went home.

Several years later, I opened my local newspaper, The St. Petersburg Times, to see that Sam was playing a club date in town the next night. Dave had died, and Sam was singing on his own. Believe it or not, with all the traveling I did with my entertainers, I did not like to go to clubs by myself. I was used to being in a group, so for me to go to a club by myself was not the norm. But, when I saw that Sam was going to play at this club for one night only, I decided that I had to go, even alone. I just had to hear his music.

My babysitter showed up, and off to the club I went. The place was packed, standing room only at the back of the room. I began to inch my way along the back wall trying to get a good place so I could see the stage. I was literally backing my way down the wall and around the room. Within a few minutes, there was this darling little blond gal inching her way behind me trying to reach the side of the stage for a good vantage point. I just missed hitting the wall sconce, but not so for the tiny blond behind me. She whacked her head soundly. I thought she was going to fall down, so I immediately turned to help her. As she was holding her head, I said to her, "let me go find some ice for you and a place for you to sit down." I was afraid that she was going to pass out. She was very calm and said that she knew where to get ice, but thanked me for stopping to assist her. There was just something about this charming woman that pulled me to her. I just knew that she had something to do with the show, so I asked her about it. She confirmed that she was. I told her that I was an old friend of Sam's and asked her to take a hello note to him that I had written on my business card. She took one look at the business card, immediately hugged me, and said she and Sam had been talking about me that very morning. I was totally dumbfounded! This woman that I had befriended was none other than Sam Moore's wife, Joyce. I could not believe my ears when she told me that Sam had never forgotten my kindness to him years ago during the Sha Na Na tour. When they were preparing to come to his St. Petersburg appearance, he had told her about me and had wondered if I would come to see him. I was blown away by this revelation. Joyce told me she was going backstage to get some ice for her head and would tell Sam, and that I should stay put at the club until the crowds left so that we could visit. I was elated.

His set was marvelous, as usual. I enjoyed the music and noticed that Sam looked so much healthier than when I had last seen him. Long after the show, Sam came out and gave me the biggest bear hug. The three of us had the greatest visit. Sam and Joyce were staying in Tampa, and we made plans for me to bring the children over to Tampa the next day after school to continue our visit. The next day, Melanie, Corbett, and I went to the hotel to have an early dinner out, all of us together. We laughed, visited, and had a great time. It was surreal to me; Sam and his wife were my friends.

A few nights later, Sam was singing at a club in Orlando, and I vowed to come to sit with Joyce during the performance. Since the Orlando show was late, I got a babysitter for the children and drove over to the club. Joyce and I were sitting there watching Sam perform, and I was loving every minute. When he started singing I Thank You, I turned to Joyce and told her that it was almost impossible to sit and not dance, because this song has so much soul. Joyce said, "Hey, let's dance!" To the bottom of the stage she and I went while Sam sang. She and I danced our hearts out. When the verse came up, "you didn't have to love me, but you did and you did and I thank you," Joyce and I pointed up to Sam and continued dancing merrily. Sam was just watching us, shaking his head. In between the music and lyrics, he called down to us from the stage and asked us to sit down. He could not concentrate on his music, because he was laughing at us. During the next break between the verses and the music, Sam again said, "I am serious. You have to sit down. I am dying laughing up here watching the two of you. I can't sing like this." Joyce and I sat down, laughing all the way. As I look back on great memories, this is truly one of the best, imagining Sam Moore cracking up on stage during one of the best songs ever! Joyce and I spent the rest of the night tapping our feet on the floor and tapping our fingers on the table. No more distractions in front of the stage for this Soul Man.

These times with Sam and Joyce cemented our friendship throughout all these many years. I have had the pleasure of being able to pick the phone up to call them, chat about music, life, children, and mutual music friends. To this day, Sam always asks about my children who are well grown up now. I think my retirement from cooking surprised him; he always asked how my business was doing. I ask about their children too. Sam keeps saying that he's going to retire. I personally hope that he is able to keep singing. A world without his wonderful personality, wit, and beautiful music would be a very different world for me. When I see Sam on television, I leave him a voice message telling him how wonderful he looks and how much I loved the performance. I feel so lucky to call Sam Moore my friend.

I adore his album, Overnight Sensational. When you hear the music and discover all the other wonderful entertainers that came into the studio to sing with him, you really realize what a wonderful force Sam has been in this crazy music business. Sam is a wonderful gift to us music lovers. He is loved and respected by his peers, and they still make the music with him. When you read about his career achievements, you realize how very loved this man is and how many lives he has touched with his music. He is a Grammy-award winner. He has appeared on every major television show in the United States. He has been featured in almost every major newspaper in the United States and featured worldwide on radio. He has been called to perform by our Presidents of the United States and Kings and Queens of the world. Sam has been inducted into the Rock and Roll Hall of Fame.

In the spring of 2010, I opened my newspaper to see that Sam Moore would be playing at the Strawberry Festival in Plant City, along with Bill Medley of the Righteous Brothers. I could not call Joyce fast enough to let her know that I would definitely be coming to the show. I was counting down the days until the concert.

The day of the show arrived, and off to Plant City I went with my husband, Ray, in tow. Sam and Joyce looked fabulous as I introduced them to Ray, and we exchanged hugs and greetings. Besides Sam's hair being shorter and whiter, he looked healthy and happy. He asked about Melanie and Corbett. While we were catching up, Bill Medley came walking by. To my surprise, Sam hollered out for him to join us and said he had a friend he wanted introduce him to. That friend was me! Oh, my goodness, there before me stood the ever-handsome Bill Medley whom I had never met nor heard live in concert. I must admit, sorry husband, but my little heart skipped a beat! After a brief conversation, Bill left our little group to get ready for the start of the show, and then Sam also disappeared.

I begged Joyce to let me stand by the side of the stage, my favorite spot, to watch Sam's set. As the original Blues Brother, Sam Moore, took the stage, I was in absolute hog heaven. Sam sang his set, and several thoughts ran through my mind. First and foremost, the man still had his pipes. There are many beloved older entertainers whose voices have faded. We go to see them in concert to relive those older days, but in reality, they cannot sing like they used to. I stood by the stage that night, listening to Sam Moore, and his pipes sounded so great to me. The next realization I had was that I could not listen to Sam and not dance, still! So there I was, some forty-four years after high school, dancing behind the curtain, while Sam was singing on stage. What a moment for me! I was loving every minute of every song. The most surprising part of the evening was when Sam came rushing off the stage. As he hurried past me, his parting words were, "Midge, I love ya honey, but you still can't dance." It takes a true friend to say that to another friend! I laughed so hard. I always thought I was a pretty good dancer in my youth, but not so much now. I still thought I was OK! Well, according to my friend, I have not ever been a great dancer, but I have loved every minute of trying.

Sam jumped into his waiting car to leave the fair grounds, and we made arrangements for Melanie to call him the next day before he left Florida. He insisted that he needed to get caught up with her and make sure she was alright after having just heard about her divorce. The following day, as I sat in my daughter's office while she and Sam visited on the phone, I was continually thinking about the amazing career that I have had.

In the summer of 2010, I got another big surprise. Joyce e-mailed me that she was putting together a surprise birthday celebration for Sam. She wanted me to mark my calendar. All I could think was "Wow." A few weeks later, I received the cutest invitation inviting me to Sam's Surprise 75th Birthday. It was to be a two-night celebration in Washington, DC. The first night would be a private dinner party, and the second was to be a roast. The roast part made me laugh out loud. As Joyce put it, "we are going to roast him like a marshmallow on the Capitol steps." I immediately made my plane and hotel reservations, pinching myself the entire time, because I was so lucky to be invited. As I was well into writing this book, I decided to keep a diary about this trip, a luxury that I did not have during my days on the road.

I flew from Chattanooga, Tennessee to Washington, D.C. on October 12, 2010. I was so looking forward to the first surprise dinner that Joyce was giving Sam that night. As a I checked in to Mansion on O Street, I ran into Joyce. She was thrilled, because so far she had been able to keep this two day event a secret from Sam. The real whammy was that Sam would think this dinner was the only party. In actuality, the biggest surprise was the comic roast on the second night, with many more people attending, and it would be filmed by the Rolling Stone Magazine.

Mansion on O Street consists of four connected brownstones. Each room has its own design with many private hideaway spots. Privacy is the big selling point to guests. When I checked in, I was assigned a secret code name. I was now "Midge Octagon." Anyone calling me at the hotel would be required to use my secret code name. As I was given the tour, I was told that everything in the hotel was for sale, down to the thousands of books throughout the hotel. If I fell in love with the chandelier that was hanging in my bedroom, I could buy it. If I liked the knick-knack that I saw on a shelf in passing, I could purchase it, no problem. The Octagon Room, also known as the Rosa Parks Room, is where that historic woman always stayed when she came to Washington, D.C. The octagonal room was painted light blue with white lace curtains on all the windows. A huge crystal chandelier hung in the middle of the bedroom, with another chandelier hanging in the bathroom. The bathroom totally knocked me out. A huge teak Jacuzzi tub with adjoining teak vanity and gleaming tile greeted me. Books lined the shelf over the tub in case I wanted to read while soaking and whirling. I couldn't contain myself; I saw a lovely, relaxing whirlpool in my near future before going out to dinner! Dinner was at the Palms at 7 pm. I had just enough time to jump into the tub.

As Sam arrived at the Palms banquet room, he was surprised to see 40 of his closest friends. Everyone took turns congratulating him and wishing him happy birthday. You could tell by the look on his face that he was indeed shocked and surprised. The conversation throughout dinner was loud and noisy, with lots of laughter and people having a wonderful time. At the close of the dinner, a big birthday cake with candles was carried into the room, and a loud Happy Birthday was sung by all.

As our dinner party came to an end, I had the restaurant call me a taxicab. I had promised my children that I would not walk back to the hotel after dark. This night was just a gorgeous night in D.C., and I was so excited to be there. I had the cab driver drive me all over downtown sight-seeing that night before going back to the hotel.

Sam's second surprise party was scheduled for six o'clock on night two. I made sure that I got to spend lots of time in my teak Jacuzzi before getting dressed for the roast.

As I entered the second floor, I was not as stranger as the previous night, because I would be seeing some of the people that I had met the night before. I picked up a martini at the bar and moved into the banquet room to find my seat. The tables were set with black tablecloths, white lace overlays, and cookie centerpieces shaped as guitars and stars. Each place setting was decorated for the Soul Man with black hats, glittering microphones, and the ever-present black sunglasses. A large screen was behind the head table. When Sam entered the room, he was totally flabbergasted. More people were there than the night before, and he was speechless except for saying to his wife, "pay backs," and we all laughed.

The buffet dinner was fabulous. I have never seen so many items offered on a single buffet. One person could not sample everything! Believe me, I tried and could not fit it on my plate, nor in my stomach. Forget about trying to go back for seconds. I grinned when I saw the peach cobbler on the dessert table. The conversation was lively, and laughter prevailed throughout the dinner service.

The roast began. As roasts go, it was hysterical with lots of jokes, and the big screen played birthday messages from friends that could not attend. There were tributes from Sting, Jordin Sparks, and Nancy Lieberman, to name a few. I learned a lot more about Sam that night and laughed myself silly, along with the entire room. One of the funniest things I have ever seen was when a hypnotist came out and convinced Sam that he was Bruce Springsteen. Another birthday cake was presented, and Sarah Dash again sang Happy Birthday to Sam. I could not help but lead the room in a standing ovation and clapping wildly at the end of her birthday song.

When it came time for Sam to speak, he began telling stories about the various people in the room. At some point, he pointed to me. I was floored and did not see this one coming. I was sitting there with my Blue's Brother hat and sunglasses. Sam proceeded to tell the room the story about how he and I had met at that Sha Na Na concert so many years ago. I could hardly breathe as the room turned their attention to me while Sam told his story -- our story. Hearing him recount it totally humbled me, and I have told my friends about it for years. He ended by adding how people taking care of each other can leave an indelible mark on a person's memory, and can actually change a life. Sam called it a random act of kindness that he never forgot.

The last night of Sam's birthday party was so vibrant, I had a hard time sleeping. I kept pinching myself during the night, because I couldn't believe that I had actually been part of such a memorable celebration for such a super star. To have the opportunity to meet so many new people was exciting all by itself. My mind was racing, leaping all around the Rosa Parks bedroom until the morning light peeped through the curtains.

As I flew back to the mountains, the last two days seemed like a dream. Sam is one of the nicest people you could ever meet. I adore Sam and his wife, Joyce. I never would have thought as a teenager, dancing in a teen club, that I would get the chance to be friends with the singer of the song I loved to dance to. I am so fortunate. Thank you, dear friend, The Great Sam Moore, for giving such fabulous music to the world. I will Dance On -- even though you say I can't.

Midge and Sam at his second night Surprise Birthday "Roast", Washington, DC

Joyce and Sam Moore and Midge at his first Surprise Birthday party in Washington, DC

Scalloped Potatoes

Always a pleaser with ham or meatloaf.

– Serves 10-12 –

◇◇

6 tbsp butter

4 tbsp all-purpose flour

3 tsp salt

¼ tsp pepper

3 c half & half

1 medium onion, diced

12 medium potatoes, sliced thinly, you can peel these or, leave the skins on as all the vitamins are in the skins.

◇◇

If you slice your potatoes before you make your sauce, keep them in salted cold water so that they will not turn brown, otherwise, make sauce first, then prepare potatoes. If your potatoes have been in salted water, make sure to drain thoroughly and pat dry.

Grease with butter a deep baking dish or use a deep disposable full metal baking dish. Support bottom with cookie sheet, this will also prevent any spillage from messing up your oven. Take your first five ingredients, put in a saucepan over medium heat, stirring so as not to burn the bottom. If you want to make au gratin potatoes, add 16 oz. package of shredded sharp or mild cheddar, which ever you prefer. Layer half your potatoes and half of your onion in the dish, pour half of your sauce over potatoes. Repeat. If you are a cheese lover, sprinkle the top with a thin layer of shredded cheddar (too much cheese could burn, be careful).

Cover with foil and bake at 350° for at least one hour. Uncover and bake for another ½ hour or until potatoes are done.

Another variation is that when you uncover your potatoes, open a can of those French-fried onions and sprinkle on the top for the last half hour bake. I know that the idea of a metal pan might sound terrible to you but, you need to use a deep dish to cook your potatoes in. Nothing is going to be worse than to have this spill over into your oven. You can always cook your dish on a cookie sheet for protection, just make sure your baking dish is nice and deep.

Midge Trubey

Chicken Piccata

Dear Sam reminded me he had eaten this at his birthday party, so, Sam, this is for you.

– Serves 6 –

12 boneless, skinless chicken tenderloins (veal can be substituted for veal Piccata)

½ tsp pepper

½ tsp garlic powder

2 eggs, beaten

2 tsp milk

1 c flour

1 tbsp butter + 1 tbsp margarine

2 tbsp oil

¼ c fresh lemon juice

4 tbsp capers, drained

1 c white wine or a little more

Flatten your chicken between two layers of plastic with a mallet or the side of a hammer. Sprinkle with pepper and garlic. Whisk egg and milk together. Dip chicken in egg mixture, coat in flour. Have ½ of your butter/margarine/oil mixture melted in a skillet over medium heat. Sauté chicken for 4-5 minutes on each side, until cooked through. Set aside chicken and keep warm. If in the middle of cooking your chicken, you need more butter/margarine/mixture, melt and continue cooking your chicken. Do not let your chicken drippings in the pan turn an ugly dark brown, watch your temperature. When all your chicken is cooked, place chicken on a dish at the side of your stove, cover with foil to keep warm while you finish the last step. To your skillet with all the drippings in it, add your wine, lemon juice and capers. Simmer until well blended, your mixture should thicken slightly. Pour over your chicken and place fresh lemon slices and fresh parsley on your dish. Serve immediately with rice, wild rice or a rice blend. I have sometimes placed my chicken in a buttered dish with the rice already fixed and then pour the yummy wine sauce over the rice. I have been known to also dot the top of my rice with little pads of butter, place the warm chicken, then the wine sauce.

Apple Horseradish Sauce

A must have with beef tenderloin. This has been a huge family favorite for years. If you are having company, you might want to double up on this recipe.

~~~

1 c of mayonnaise (Hellman's or Dukes)

1 medium whole red apple

1 regular slice of sweet onion

½ c drained prepared horseradish

1 tbsp of fresh lemon juice

Sprinkle of white pepper

Fresh dill to taste (optional if not a dill fan but this makes the sauce. I have used dried dill when I could not get my hands on fresh)

~~~

Core your red apple, leave skin on and chunk, put into your food processor, pulse to make chunks (do not liquefy) and transfer to a small mixing bowl). Put onion into food processor, pulse to small pieces, add to apples in mixing bowl. Add lemon juice to apples and mix thoroughly. Add mayonnaise, horseradish, and white pepper. Use spatula to mix thoroughly. (If you want hotter seasoning, add more horseradish) Add dill to taste, depending on how you like dill. Blend all together and refrigerate until ready to use.

Midge Trubey

85

Peach Cobbler

One of Sam's Favorites

∞∞

1 stick of butter

1 c of self-rising flour

¾ c sugar or Splenda

¾ c milk

2 c of fresh sliced peaches (can use your "fruit of choice")

¼ c sugar or Splenda (you can add a dash of cinnamon if you like that flavor)

∞∞

Preheat oven to 350°. Melt butter in a shallow 1 ½-quart baking dish. In mixing bowl, mix the flour, ¾ sugar and milk, get the lumps out. Pour evenly over the melted butter. Combine ¼ sugar and your peaches or berries or apples and cinnamon (if you wish for peaches and apples). Spoon evenly over the flour mixture. Do not stir. Bake approximately 40-45 minutes or until the top is lightly browned. Serve with vanilla ice cream or fresh whipped cream.

Ratatouille

This was a hit when the movie Health was filmed in St. Petersburg.

– Serves 12 –

2 medium eggplant, diced unpeeled

3 zucchinis, half sliced

3 yellow squash, half sliced

4 medium Vidalia onions, diced

8 medium red bliss potatoes, quartered

2 medium green peppers, cleaned and diced

2 - 16 oz cans Italian plum tomatoes, undrained, squish the tomatoes through your hands

4 cloves garlic, crushed

2 tsp fresh basil

1 tsp dried oregano

2 tbsp salt

½ tsp freshly ground black pepper

1 c olive oil

Combine all vegetables in large bowl. Add cans of tomatoes and all seasonings, mix thoroughly. Add olive oil last, mix thoroughly, turning mixture whereby all ingredients are coated evenly. Gently place in large heavy pot on top of stove, cook slowly uncovered 1 ½ hours, stirring occasionally. Turn stove off, allow to stand for several hours. Can be served hot or cold.

Midge Trubey

Baked Stuffed French Toast With Praline Topping

Our family favorite for all brunch gatherings.

1 loaf of French bread or bread of choice (raisin bread or challah work great)

2-8 oz packages of cream cheese, room temperature

¼ c of your favorite jam i.e. strawberry, marmalade, blueberry (if you do not want flavored filling, just add sugar to taste to your cream cheese or leave cream cheese out altogether)

8 eggs

2 c of half & half

1 c milk

2 tbsp sugar or Splenda

1 tsp vanilla

½ tsp cinnamon

¼ tsp nutmeg

Dash of salt

<u>For Praline topping:</u>

1 c (2 sticks) of butter, melted

1 c light brown sugar, packed (can use Splenda brown sugar)

1 c chopped pecans

2 tbsp light corn syrup

½ tsp cinnamon

½ tsp nutmeg

Baked Stuffed French Toast With Praline Topping (cont)

Preheat oven to 350. Slice bread into about 20 slices, each approximately 1 inch thick. Set aside. Mix together the cream cheese at room temperature and jam until well mixed and smooth. Make sandwiches with your bread, arrange sandwiches in a generously buttered deep dish baking dish, overlapping of slices is OK.

In a large bowl, combine eggs, half and half, milk, sugar, vanilla, cinnamon, nutmeg and salt. Whisk until blended but not too bubbly. Pour mixture over bread slices, making sure all are covered, even spoon some of the mixture between the slices. Let egg mixture seep in for about 15 minutes. You can refrigerate baking dish overnight, just cover with foil.

Before you put baking dish into your oven, make the praline topping by combining all the topping ingredients, spread evenly over the bread mixture. Put your baking dish on a cookie sheet before you put into the oven. Bake uncovered for 45 minutes if mixture is already at room temperature. If baking dish is coming out of refrigerator cold, remove foil, baking time will be at least one hour long.

Your dish will be fully cooked when puffed in the center and has turned a light brown color. Serve with maple syrup.

Midge Trubey

Going National

I believe by now, anyone reading this book knows that I consider myself a very lucky woman. The Personal Touch was in business six weeks after I had my first brochure printed with my original idea. Within a matter of six months, I was cooking throughout the state of Florida. Before I even hit my two-year business anniversary, I was cooking on a national tour. Newspaper and magazine articles were being written about my business. Television coverage was not far behind. When I started the company in 1977, I would have never predicted the vast scope of the company. In a short period of time, my reputation for providing home cooked meals with efficiency and care was beyond my wildest dreams. Unfortunately, another family situation had to be dealt with.

My husband, Dennis, had been ready for a divorce even before I started The Personal Touch, something that he had not shared with me. I was working for us when there was no us. The business did not help our relationship. In looking back, I am thankful for Dennis for standing by me during the time it took to develop the business, thus making our divorce easier on the both of us financially. We have remained friends throughout all these years, and there are several points we agree on. We were married young; we had been high school sweethearts. We both feel that fact really worked against us; we were too young. I found out years later that no one in the family was more surprised about the scope of my business success than Dennis. But here I was, divorced with two beautiful children, and not working a traditional nine-to-five job in the same city as my kids.

While the company was developing, I was not working every week. The concerts were spaced so that I could find someone to help me with my children. My mother was mortified about my job, and she staunchly refused to baby sit. My father in law loved to baby sit, but my mother in law did not. Dennis was working his own job. I felt frustration like any mother with children who is going to work, no matter the age. As Dennis and I divorced, taking good care of my children was my number one priority, plus I needed to support myself and have the money to raise my children. I wanted to provide for them in the manner in which I was provided for as a child. We were not a rich family growing up, but my parents worked hard to raise four daughters. I was the eldest child in the family, and I always appreciated them for the opportunities afforded me.

Back when I was on tour with all these different people, there were no cell phones or computers. We were a technically-isolated group moving down the road together, relying on each other and concert venues for a telephone connection to the outside world. My connection to my family was any payphone that I could find. I never thought of using the production office telephone for any personal calls. That phone was the only means of communication to solidify upcoming dates and arrangements for the tour while we were moving around the country.

My next-door neighbor's high-school aged daughter was my regular babysitter, but the first woman to help me when I started traveling was actually my daughter's elementary school teacher. She was unmarried, loved children (particularly mine), and we became great friends. Years later, she became one of the most-admired school principals in our county, and I am most thankful for her to this day.

When the traveling picked up to the national level, and this dear woman got engaged to her darling husband, I needed to find someone else to help me with the kids. Again, I was so fortunate to have neighbors with two children the same age as mine. When I would get the call to do a show, I could contact them, pack up my children's little suitcases, and take them over to their home. As two families, we had the same discipline rules and a lot of love for our children. I could come home from a show (or multiple shows), and I did not have to retrain my children. When I came home, I always looked forward to spending quality time with my them and continuing on with their school schedule and outside activities. Continuity and a stable environment with lots of love have always been my primary concern. My job was demanding, and I needed to concentrate on my work when I was at work, not worrying about my children. When I was home, I liked nothing better than being the normal mom, cleaning my house, carpooling and participating in school outings, and cooking dinners for my children. Florida is a great place to raise kids, with plenty of parks, gorgeous beaches, and wonderful weather to enjoy year-round. To this day, my grown children love the outdoors. I also found out that my children had a natural curiosity about what Mom was doing at work. As the months of business progressed, I realized that I could actually take them to some of these shows, working around their school schedules. The two of them grew up backstage at family shows. I knew these family-oriented concerts would not expose them to the sex and drugs that accompany some shows. Notice, I said "some." There were many family-oriented concerts during this time. Many entertainers projected family images, and their alcohol and drug use was not flaunted for all to see. Melanie was in elementary school, so I would not deviate from her school schedule. If she could go with me for the day on a weekend, I would take her. She was always willing to help wash dishes and follow me around. The look of wonder on her face when the entertainers took the stage at night was priceless. Plus, she was with me, and I felt good about that. My little boy was just in preschool. I missed him terribly when I was not home, and I knew from experience how much I was missing in his development. So, I took Corbett with me as much as possible. He was the best child backstage. The guys could not believe that he would be so content coloring next to the stove almost the entire day while I cooked. I could always take some time to color or play with him. He has colored with some of the biggest names in the entertainment industry. Chrissie Hynde of the Pretenders spent an afternoon coloring with Corbett in between sound check in Port St. Lucie. My daughter remembers seeing coloring books with Joan Jett and Michael Jackson's name written on different pictures. I wish I could find those coloring books!

The drum roadies would let Corbett watch the drums being set up on stage. They would ask him to sit in one place and watch. After a little while, the guys would inevitably come to tell me they couldn't believe how well-behaved he was. Corbett would just sit there soaking up the work and chatting with the guys. Since he was so little, I would make him a bed by my stove, and when he got tired, I would tuck him in to sleep right there in my work area. Imagine, sound blazing with all the noise, and there was my son, sound asleep. Rock babies can sleep through anything; just ask any musician who had children. My son and daughter were happiest being with me, and I felt lucky taking them with me whenever I could. Unconventional? Definitely. But this was our family lifestyle. There were so many weekends when my children traveled with me.

Journey

Little did I know when I met Journey, along with Ronnie Montrose and Van Halen, back in 1978, how this band would impact my life. Journey was the first band that asked me to go on national tour with them. Everything started out great! We began the tour in Passaic, New Jersey, went up to Maine, down to Texas, up through California, and over to Nevada. By the time we got to Nevada 6 weeks later, I was fired. I was taken to the airport with my stove, refrigerator, and pots and pans box, then flown home. How did this happen?

Life on the road is brutal. There is no time for illness. The food gets served, the show goes on, no exceptions. Unfortunately, I'm prone to pneumonia and upper-respiratory infections. By the time we hit Corpus Christi, Texas, I had come down sick with a vengeance and knew I had to go to the emergency room. As the ER doctor told me to take pills and go home to bed, I remember laughing hysterically. First, I really didn't have a bed, I could not go home, and I could not stop to rest. He listened to me and then told me to bend over; he was going to give me a shot that would help. To this day, I wish I knew what was in that shot! I really don't remember much of the next three days, except that Holly and I got fired. I know I was working, and I remember the crew laughing at me, but that is about all. Years later, I was in Corpus Christi, Texas, again with Molly Hatchett. The local crew still remembered me, bouncing off the walls over how sick I had been. Wow, talk about going down in flames! To say I was disappointed would be an understatement, but I was going home to my children, so that going to be okay.

Was that experience a complete bust for me? Absolutely not. First of all, I left loving every single person involved with that organization. I had no idea some of these men would become lifelong friends. I left on good terms. The experiences I had were amazing, such as Steve Perry cooking with me on a fire escape in downtown Boston with hundreds of screaming girls down below. The building was so old, no cooking was allowed on the inside. I cooked on a loading dock in Long Beach as the building would not let my stove inside. Going to a Bill Graham Day on The Green production in Oakland was iconic. I learned so much. Every new experience expanded my vision of what my company could become. No one ever likes to get fired, but when one door closes, another one opens.

To this day, when Journey tours, I am there as their guest. We share stories and pictures of the past. My husband stays in shock, as does my son-in-law, when my Melanie and I hop around the venue visiting and laughing. It never pays to burn your bridges; you never know what the future will hold. I still love Journey and their music. I totally loved my latest visit with the band when Ross asked "Midge, where is the food?" I brought out my old pictures of that short time in 1978, and they were a huge hit. What a grin!

Steve Smith and I have stayed friends all these years. What a delightful, talented man. To renew old friendships is also such a blessing. I asked Scotty "So, what have you been doing the last 40+ years?" Lots of laughter, memories, and catching up is always great. All the Journey men are still so kind and funny. They warm my heart. If Journey had not sent me home, I would have missed out on the friendship of my lifetime, the great Kenny Rogers.

Midge, Steve Smith with his child on sightseeing day trip to Napa Valley, 1985. I was advancing Super Bowl in Palo Alto, Ca

Recent picture of Midge and Ross Vallory talking about the "the good ol' days', Tampa Florida

Recent picture of Midge, Steve Smith ad wife, Debbie, reminiscing at promo pictures from 1978

Pat Trubey's Burgundy Stew

Serve a nice crusty bread and butter with this one. You'll want to slurp the bread and butter with the gravy!

— Serves 6-8 —

3 lbs of stew meat, trimmed of any gristle

1 medium sweet onion, quartered and sliced

1 pt of mushrooms, sliced

4-6 red bliss potatoes, cut into bite sized pieces, do not peel, clean thoroughly

4-6 carrots, cut into bite sized pieces, do not peel, you will miss your vitamins, clean thoroughly

One can of Campbell's tomato soup

Burgundy wine

Dried basil

Salt, pepper and garlic powder to taste

Put into your crock pot, sprinkle liberally with flour. Add one can of tomato soup. Add equal can of burgundy wine. Pour a little dried basil into the palm of your hand, crush and roll in your hands and add to your stew. Crock pot on low for about 4-5 hours, or until your meat is tender. The beauty of this recipe is that you do not brown the meat ahead of time. I stir this mixture about twice while it is cooking. I have also made this on top of my stove, cooked on low for about 3 hours. I have also cooked this in my oven at 325° for three hours. Stir whichever way you are cooking.

Midge Trubey

Beer Bread

Great with chili or soups!

<><><><><><><><><><><><><><><><><><><><><><><><><><><><><><><><><><>

3 c self-rising flour	1 - 12 oz. can of beer	3 tbsp sugar

<><><><><><><><><><><><><><><><><><><><><><><><><><><><><><><><><><>

Blend together the flour and sugar in a mixing bowl, add the beer, blend well. Pour into a loaf pan that is greased on the sides with waxed paper bottom. Cook 375° for 1 ½ hours.

Quick Chicken Curry

*Quick, easy, and everyone loves playing
with all the various toppings.*

1 large onion

2 tbsp margarine/
butter
combination

3 – 10.5 oz cans of
cream of
mushroom soup

¾ c whole milk

1 ½ tsp curry
powder

3 c cooked and
cubed chicken

Chop and cook onion, in the margarine/butter combination. Add cans of cream of mushroom soup and milk, heat and stir until smooth. Stir in sour cream and curry powder. Add chicken, heat thoroughly on medium heat, do not boil. Serve with white rice, either separate or on top of rice. Garnish dish with fresh chopped parsley.

Must be served with sides of chutney, golden raisins, and toasted slivered almonds.

Midge Trubey

Pat Trubey's
Mock Quiche Lorraine

A great twist on regular pie crust.

— Serves 4 —

2 c plain croutons

1 c of shredded Swiss cheese

<u>In mixing bowl, combine:</u>

2 c whole milk

4 slightly beaten eggs

½ tsp salt

½ tsp prepared mustard

⅛ tsp onion powder

Dash of pepper

Mix until blended and pour over croutons.

Cook 6 slices of bacon crisp, crumble, sprinkle over the top. (Bacon optional)

In bottom of greased loaf pan spread out the crouton and sprinkle with swiss cheese. Pour mixed ingredients over croutons and cheese.

Bake 325° for 55-60 minutes until eggs are set.

Ross's Quick Dip

How easy is this? No one is ever able to guess what this one is.
See Ross, I never forgot!

〰〰〰〰〰〰〰〰〰〰〰〰〰〰〰〰〰〰〰〰〰〰〰〰〰〰〰〰〰〰〰

| 1 c of mayonnaise (Dukes or Hellman's) | Add ground curry powder to taste, mix well. |

〰〰〰〰〰〰〰〰〰〰〰〰〰〰〰〰〰〰〰〰〰〰〰〰〰〰〰〰〰〰〰

Mix well and surround with beautiful fresh vegetables. Ross Valory loves this in his dressing room.

Ross Vallory hosting a crew get together at his home and Ross working, 1978

Midge Trubey

The Legend, Kenny Rogers

In the late 70s, I was lucky enough to be introduced to the wonderful and exciting world of Kenny Rogers. For almost two years, I crisscrossed the country twice with this multi-talented entertainer. Kenny Rogers was definitely "it" in songs, entertainment, and movies during the 70s and 80s. After the national tours, I continued working for him until I retired. Our friendship carried on until he passed away in 2020.

It was always a wonderful pleasure to see my boss along with the band and his trusted road crew after I retired whenever they were on tour. The entire day would be filled with lots of talking and nostalgia, something I could not do back in the day when I was working. To catch Kenny Rogers when he was not surrounded by tons of people was almost impossible, but I always did. I want to share with you a little of our conversation from a day in 2009.

The band was warming up in a corner room of the backstage area in the concert hall. I came whipping in to listen, not noticing Kenny sitting in a chair back from the door. As I blundered in, Kenny immediately stood up to give me one of his great hugs and invited me to "sing in" as he said, "you know all the words." I reminded him that some things never change: I knew all the words, but I still couldn't carry a tune in a bucket, which brought remembered laughs from Kenny and his band. After this mini rehearsal, I caught up with Kenny. I told him I was writing this book. In his witty style, Kenny told me that he was beyond worrying about what people write about him and for me to have a ball writing whatever I saw fit to print. I reminded him that it was all good stuff, as we were such a large family, continually playing practical jokes on each other as we rumbled down the highways. Kenny turned to me, looking me straight in the eyes, and said, "yes, we were very lucky; it was a great time in our lives."

During the two years I traveled with Kenny, the tour sold out every night in huge stadiums from Maine to Texas, Michigan to New Mexico, and Arizona to Florida. The man was hot. Kenny was the silver-haired king turning everything he touched into gold. Everyone who worked for Kenny Rogers knew that we had the responsibility of producing one of the hottest concerts of our era. The people that clamored to see his shows expected to see the best. The pressure was on all of us to produce and do our jobs the best, or you were not asked back. It was our duty to take care of our boss and to protect him from his adoring and sometimes overzealous fans. I witnessed middle-age women breaking their arms and legs just to touch him as he passed through the audience to get to his stage in the round. Kenny would be surrounded by security guards. It did not matter; people just wanted to touch him. I saw grown men dress as Kenny Rogers and grow their hair and beards to match his. We called them "Kenny Clones." There were plenty of times that all of us in the entourage would take a double look at these men who liked to get as close to the backstage area as they could.

THE KENNY ROGERS SHOW
FOOD REQUIREMENTS

All of the attached food requirements are to be cleared by our office contact, Debbie Cross. This would consist of caterer, menu items and food costs, also, including tax, labor and gratuity (if any).

Please call Debbie Cross in C. K. Spurlock's office at 615-822-1817 with your total price for all of the food requirements and your meat selection plus vegetables for the crew dinner. The food information sheet that is enclosed will be of help to the caterer on figuring his cost. It is also of great help to Debbie if the caterer can promptly fill out this sheet and r___ it to her so that she will have a copy for her files.

___ meals that we request for the crew includes our people ___rs, riggers, stagehands, etc.) so please do not ___an the quantities we have requested.

Debbie Cross   10-11-84

___ add eight (8) meals to our ___two shows on the same ___up prior to the ___see if any

___iate it if ___er, between

___rew breakfast, ___st show day. ___inner are to be

___ we have two shows

___enny Rogers show do ___use you call ___er you do or do not

___ us we will be needing ___anager, Tim Rogers. We ___ towel requirements. If ___m Rogers by 4:00 PM could ___ing room for Gene Roy,

Midge:
Here are the food require- ments for Kenny, Crystal, Sawyer Brown and Rabbitt. Sylvia will be on the later Dec. dates - or she may not even be on them at all. The venue info is enclosed also. Let me know if you have any questions.
Re: budget, Let me know what fee. We'll run it past CK
Thanks,

Midge Trubey

Letter and note from Debbie Cross, my forever Kenny Rogers friend and "go to" back in the day

KENNY ROGERS TOUR - 1981

Friday - Jan. 9, 1981 - Austin Univer. Spec. Ev. Cen. , Austin, Tx. - 18,000 approx. seats

Saturday - Jan. 10, 1981 - Tarrant Cty. Conv. Cen., Ft. Worth, Tx. - 13,956 approx. seats

Sunday - Jan. 11, 1981 - Barton Col., Little Rk., Ark. - 10,012 approx. seats

Tuesday - Jan. 13, 1981 - Kansas Col., Wichita, Kan. - 12,000 approx. seats

Thursday - Jan. 15, 1981 - L'loyd Noble Cen., Norman, Okla. - 13,000 approx. seats

Friday - Jan. 16, 1981 - Amarrilo Civ. Cen., Amarrilo, Tx. - 7,500 approx. seats

Saturday - Jan. 17, 1981 - New Mex. Univ. Spec. Ev. Cen., Las Cruces, N. Mex. - 13,958 seats

Sunday - Jan. 18, 1981 - Tuson Comm. Cen., Tuson, Ariz. - 9,550 approx. seats

April 14 - Johnson City, Tenn., Freedom Hall,
April 15 - Augusta, GA, dbl. show - 5:30 - 8:30 - Augusta Civic Center
April 16 - Macon GA.

Thursday - April 30, 1981 - Stokley Bldg., Univer. of Tn., Knoxville, Tn. - 13,200 approx.seat

Friday - May 1, 1981 - Rupp Arena, Lexington, Ky. - 23,000 approx. seats

Saturday - May 2, 1981 - Charleston Civ. Cen., Charleston, W. Va. - 13,670 approx. seats

Sunday - May 3, 1981 - Roanoke Civ. Cen., Roanoke, Va. - 11,000 approx. seats

Tuesday - May 5, 1981 - Richmond Col., Richmond, Va. - 11,971 approx. seats

Wednesday - May 6, 1981 - Washington, Capitol Cen., - 19,000 approx. seats

Thursday - May 7, 1981 - Hampton Col. Arena, Hampton, Va. - 12,075 approx. seats

Friday - May 8, 1981 - Greensboro Col., Greensboro, N.C. - 16,800 approx. seats

Saturday - May 9, 1981 - Charlotte Col., Charlotte, N.C. - 13,500 approx. seats

Sunday - May 10, 1981 - Columbia Col. Univer. of S.C., Columbia, S.C. - 13,500 approx. seats

Tuesday - May 12, 1981 - Roberts Mun. Stad., Evansville, Ind. - 13,600 approx. seats

Wednesday - May 13, 1981 - Univer. of Ind., Bloomington, Ind. - 17,000 approx. seats

Thursday - May 14, 1981 - Notre Dame Athletic & Conv. Cen., South Bend, Ind. - 12,200 app.seat

Friday - May 15, 1981 - Univer. of Ill., Champaign, Ill. - 7,900 approx. seats

Saturday - May 16, 1981 - Cent. Hall Univer. of Toleo, Toledo, Ohio - 9,866 approx. seats

Sample of how our tours started,
forever changing in those days which
was the normal

The stage was built in the middle of the concert hall, surrounded by the audience seating. For Kenny to get there safely, he had to be escorted by a wall of huge security men, walking through an aisle to get to the side steps. The stage was arranged so that the band and the crew sat and worked in the middle and that Kenny could move all around the perimeter. The interior of the stage held the band. Cordless microphones had not yet been invented, so stagehands were continually unraveling cords as Kenny roamed the stage entertaining his huge audiences. Entertaining in this style was so wildly successful for him that the following year something new was added. Four screens would drop down simultaneously at each corner to show scenes of the Gambler while he sang the song. This visual show was wildly popular with the audiences. What was not popular with Kenny was that sometimes one or more of the screens would get stuck, and the four would not come down at the same time as they were supposed to. This did not make him very happy. These screens were very delicate, and the daily packing and unpacking took a toll on the equipment. The pressure was on. It was a common practice for all of us backstage to come running with bets in hand to see if the screens would drop correctly at the proper time with the song. I won a few bets and lost a few! The screens were used at another point in the show that proved to be just as popular as the Gambler sequence. Kenny and his then wife, Marianne, had been recently blessed with this darling baby boy, Christopher. Much to the delight of the audience, baby pictures of this beautiful little boy were shown while Kenny sang one of his hits. One of the most charismatic aspects of Kenny Rogers is that he always shared his personal life with his audiences.

Kenny always had a great sense of humor, true wit, and was extremely congenial, but Kenny guarded his privacy. He surrounded himself with people that protected him and respected him, not only for his talent, but for being the human being that he was. I was lucky to be on the fringes of this inner circle. My job was to provide breakfast, lunch, dinner, sound check food, and dressing room food for approximately 50-60 people. There would be nights when I fixed a snack for Kenny to take on the plane as he flew back to the farm. I was tasked with feeding the people of Kenny's entourage plus whoever was the opening act at that time. All local stagehands that helped produce the show were to be included also. Depending on the size of the venue, the total number of people involved with a certain production could swell to over 100 people. I also had a wonderful girl, Judy, who handled Kenny's wardrobe. As food was involved in all stages of show production, I had to talk with Kenny and his inner circle of people every day. "Had to talk" sounds so impersonal, but it was a necessity of my job to communicate daily with my boss on his likes and dislikes, as well as requests and preferences of the entire entourage.

When I was hired, I was told I only had to listen to two people: one was Kenny Rogers, and the other one was CK Spurlock, the promoter of the show. I was to take direction only from these two men. All requests made by the other people traveling on the road could be honored at my discretion, as long as it fit the budget and workload that I could carry. I would always honor a request for extra vitamins or cough medicine if someone had come down with a cold. Having a healthy crew was one of our main objectives. Another objective was "a happy crew works better together." I had to take any other requests from the crew directly to CK or Kenny to get permission before I could act. Budget was always a concern, as well as consistency and quality of the meals I was producing. The major benefit of having a traveling cook was that daily requests could be honored from the crew, such as "how about BBQ tomorrow?" or regional cooking depending on where we were in the country. I had a ball cooking with the regional food with our traveling schedule. If we were in New Orleans, I would cook Cajun. In the south, I would fix BBQ or traditional southern menus. In Maine, we had lobsters. I must tell you a lobster story.

In Portland, Maine, the local backstage building manager provided this wonderful, huge pot for boiling lobsters. All of us were just thrilled! My daily runner took me down to the lobster docks so that I could purchase some for the crew -- fifty lobsters! When Kenny arrived just before dinner, I enthusiastically informed him that we had lobsters ready to go into the pot. To my disappointment, he told me that he did not want lobster. He and Marianne wanted pizza. Pizza over lobster -- can you believe that? The crew was thrilled; more lobster for them. Pizza for the boss.

There was another time in Macon, Georgia, when I was grilling steaks for the crew just outside our secured area. Kenny would have someone call me every day to tell me how many extra people he would be bringing to dinner each night. He was very good about keeping me informed except for this one day when someone forgot to call me. Kenny and Marianne came to the venue with about six extra people. Of course I told him it was absolutely no problem. The charcoal was still very hot in the grill, and the grocery store was just around the corner. I had plenty of baked potatoes, salad, rolls, and dessert. I could have steaks on the grill and serve him and his guests within the hour. Kenny told me that this was just too much trouble. Imagine a boss telling you that? He wanted me to order pizza instead of grilling steaks. The issue at hand was getting to Pizza Hut, and then trying to get back to the venue with thousands of adoring fans arriving at the same time for the concert. Pizza Hut was nowhere near the concert arena. Kenny told me not to worry, just order the pizza, and he would have someone come get me and take me to Pizza Hut. Well, I ran to the payphone. Picture this, a woman on a pay phone, ordering pizza for Kenny Rogers, insisting that this was not a crank call but very serious business. The managers of Pizza Huts were always skeptical when they received these orders. At this time, pay phones had distinct phone numbers. When I was asked my return phone number, the manager would automatically know that I was calling from a pay phone. I would have to go in depth about the importance of this order and swear that this was not a crank call. On this particular night, I had to talk extra fast to place the order. When I turned around, there stood two Georgia state troopers to take me to get Kenny's pizza. I must tell you, this was my first and only time to be in the back seat of a police car, in the cage, with the sirens blaring to and from the pizza parlor. When we pulled up at the Pizza Hut, the manager was stunned. I paid for the order and got back into the police car. With sirens blaring, we went back to the venue with Kenny's pizzas. There may be some of you that think this was inappropriate, but back then, anyone would do anything for Kenny Rogers and be thankful to do it. It was a different time.

You never knew who Kenny and Marianne would bring with them each day to the concerts. The crew traveled each day by buses. Kenny would fly in each day from his ranch in Athens, Georgia. Kenny had many friends in various professions and fields of entertainment, as did Marianne. I never knew what each day would hold in terms of cooking requests or who would be backstage. During this time, Marianne was on the television show Hee Haw. One of her best friends was Linda Thompson and her then husband, Bruce Jenner. I would see them on a regular basis. There was one particular time when Linda came to talk with me while I was cooking at the stove. I turned to talk with her and saw the most gorgeous diamond necklace ever. You see necklaces today with people's names on them, but back then, it was not common at all. This particular necklace would never be called common. It was made of huge diamonds with her name "Linda" spelled out. Being the diamond nut I am, my mouth fell open, and I told her it was absolutely gorgeous. Linda told me, "Elvis gave it to me." I said, "Elvis! Elvis who?" Linda looked at me like I had two heads and said, "Elvis Presley, of course". She had been engaged to him and was surprised that I did not know that. Bruce would come to see what I was cooking, and talking with him was always pleasant. What an athlete! Bruce and I would have great discussions on why I was wearing the running shoes that I wore versus the shoes that he endorsed. My big feet were always important to me; I searched long and hard to find the shoes that worked best for me and my long workdays.

Another day that stands out was when the tour was in Lexington, Kentucky, the night before the Kentucky Derby in Louisville. The governor of Kentucky and his wife, former Miss America Maryanne Mobley, helicopered into the concert hall with Debbie Reynolds and Mohammed Ali. Debbie Reynolds has always been a favorite of mine, so tiny and such a talented dancer. I had always loved watching her movies and on television. What can be said about Mohammed Ali that has not been said? He was a giant of a man and so good looking. After working 12-hours, with more to go, seeing these special guests always gave you extra energy to get through the rest of the night.

One of Kenny's most special guests was always his mom. She was just a lovely lady. She would tell me that she did not know how I cooked and took care of so many people. She had the greatest smile and was so sweet. I had the pleasure of meeting Kenny's brothers, sisters, nieces, and nephews too. I really enjoyed the entire family. I got to know his brother, Lelan, the best. Lelan traveled with Kenny as his manager the last year that I worked for Kenny. Lelan was a gentle man. Kenny also had more family that traveled and worked for him, such as Paul and Tim Rogers. You just had to love the Rogers family. Truly a nice family, one and all, and not pretentious. Just down to earth people.

Once at a concert at the Capitol Center in Washington, D.C., I was bringing water and towels to the stage when I literally bumped into Harry Chapin. I had worked for Harry previously in Florida but was surprised when he recognized me. Harry and Kenny were friends. This particular night, Harry was taking the stage to promote his cause for ending world hunger asking for donation of canned goods. Harry Chapin was one of the first entertainers to promote this cause at a concert. He was just a beautiful man. Shortly after this tour, Harry was tragically killed in an automobile accident. For many years after this at Christmas time, Kenny Rogers collected the canned goods. It was his way of honoring his good friend, Harry Chapin.

I am sure that there were many more celebrities that accompanied Kenny to his shows that I did not recognize. Celebrities are just regular people, for the most part. They just have a different way of making a living from the rest of us. The aura of "being a celebrity" is glamorized day in and day out on television, magazines, newspapers, and now the Internet. I always felt that people are people; they just want to be treated as a regular person. We all get dressed the same way each day, one leg at a time. This philosophy of mine, and my desire to do the best job that I could with a smile on my face, carried me far. I never considered myself to be the best cook ever.

One night we were at the Dome in New Orleans. It was a huge night with thousands of people in the audience. It was also the last night of that particular leg of the tour. This meant that we all got to go home for a break afterward. The Dome is huge to work. To get to the dressing rooms from the crew area, I had to use a golf cart provided by the Dome. The closer it got to show time, the less available the golf carts were. Garth was Kenny's road manager at that time – no, not Garth Brooks. Kenny was already in the building when Garth came looking for me. Kenny had guests in the dressing room and needed more sparkling water. I grabbed bottles of water and hopped on the golf cart with him. Have you ever seen anybody do wheelies in a golf cart? Well, Garth did. I kept asking him to stop, because I was afraid the water would get bubbly, but he just kept running with that cart. It was funny, and we were laughing, but... When he delivered me to the dressing room, I saw Kenny sitting at the card table playing cards with three other men, a scene that was repeated on many a night. But this was the first night I had a jiggly ride to the dressing room. I stood behind Kenny to open the sparkling water to serve him and his guests. Of course, you know what happened. The water shot up and over the head of Kenny Rogers and landed on the fully-fanned cards in his hands, dripping onto the table. I thought I was going to die of embarrassment. Without even moving, he said, "Midge, that must be you behind me." I always carried a kitchen towel with me, and I began patting the cards that still had not moved from his hands, and then I began to pat the cards on the table. The room was absolutely quiet, without a peep from anyone. I just kept saying, "I am so sorry," over and over again. I told you that Kenny had a great wit. Thank God his sense of humor did not fail me that night. With a very straight face, he said that it was the end of the tour for some people that night -- and some would not be returning. I kept wiping the table and cards saying that I was looking forward to the break, but I was looking forward to coming back out for the next leg of the tour. I was so flustered that I actually asked him if I would be back. At that point, the entire room broke out laughing as Kenny said,

Midge Trubey

107

"What would I do without Midge?" I just kept cleaning up the table with my towel, mumbling "oh, thank you, thank you" while the room was laughing. I could not tell you who those other three men were playing cards with Kenny. They were just his friends, and thank God Kenny had a sense of humor. A new deck of cards was opened, I left the room, and the card came started over.

In general, the workday started at 6:30 am for me and my crew. It was our responsibility to get hot coffee and breakfast ready for the men working the 7:30 am set up call. Setting up my kitchen was always a challenge in every city every day of each tour. As this show was one of the largest productions of its day, the concert hall managers were, for the most part, very accommodating in helping me arrange my kitchen. I needed power for the stove (a pigtail to be hotwired wherever), running water close by, a room designated as "The Food Room," and an outlet for the refrigerator. I also needed tables and chairs for all the crew to be able to sit down

A typical crew meal back stage

to eat their meals together. I also required out-lets for coffee pots, teapots, and toasters. I always had to know the location of the ice machines. None of these large concert halls during this time period had kitchens to work in. I had to make my own kitchen area. All this had to be readied before any of our guys stepped off the buses to go to work. As soon as breakfast was organized, my runner would take me to the grocery store so that I could shop for the food that was needed that day. The other two girls in my crew would cook breakfast for the guys. They knew that any special requests for vitamins, cough medicine, candy, a different beer, or you name it, needed to be given to me by 8:30 am for my daily shopping trip. In the seventies, concert halls did not have washing machines. On many an occasion, Kenny's dressing room manager would give me his underwear to take to the public laundromat on my way to the grocery store. I can imagine that you are laughing, but believe me, this is true. Back then the laundromat was always next door to the grocery store. I would get the laundry started, go next door and shop, then go back to put the clothes in the dryer. Easy, the undies were done. Blue silk -- not tightie-whities. I told Kenny years later, I could have made a fortune if those women at the laundry only knew it was his underwear! Actually,

The Legend, Kenny Rogers

if those women knew it was his underwear, I would have been lucky to go back to find anything left in the washing machine or the dryer.

In the 70s, mega grocery stores like Wal-Mart or Sam's Club did not exist. It was challenging to find a store besides the smaller neighborhood ones to buy in the quantity and variety that I needed. Also, some states do not allow grocery stores to sell beer, which I needed daily. If there was no beer at the grocery store, I had to make an additional stop before going back to the arena. Finding a large grocery store was the key to my day. I needed help from these stores with the quantity and quality of food that I demanded for my men, otherwise my day would be a disaster. The butcher was important, fresh produce was a must, and I needed a deli with lots of variety, plus a big, yummy bakery. Being quick at the grocery store was a must since I was buying for lunch that day. Breakfast for the next day would also be purchased at the same time. Depending on the weather, breakfast for the next day could travel in my refrigerator to the next town, or we would pack the breakfast items in ice for the overnight trip. After getting back to the concert hall with all the groceries, the fun would really begin. It took three of us slicing, dicing, and cooking the rest of the day to produce lunch at 1:00 pm, sound check food at 4:00 pm, dinner at 6:30 pm, dressing room food at 7:00 pm, and the show to start at 8:00 pm. In between, there would always be requests for additional or changed items for the next day, plus anything extra that Kenny might want. There were times when he asked me to pack him some food to take with him after the show on the flight back to Georgia. Now, you might think with him being the icon that he was, he might request something gourmet. His most favorite request was just cheese and crackers. Velveeta cheese in slices with crackers in a little brown paper bag. "Just simple, Midge," and "thank you." Here is a man that could request literally anything, climbing the steps of his private jet with his brown paper bag of Velveeta cheese and crackers. After Kenny left the building, all the dressing rooms had to be cleared out, the rooms left respectable, equipment packed up, and then we could move on down the highway. By this time, it would be after midnight, and all to be repeated by 6:30 the next morning.

Kenny flew in from his Athens farm on most days. He would come into the building just before dinner. One day that I noticed he was running later than usual. He came into the building covered in red clay and needed to hop into the shower at the facility. He told our wardrobe gal, Judy, that he had lost track of time and had been putting up fence posts at the farm. I was entering the room as he was asking her to clean the Georgia clay off his snake-skinned boots while he was on stage. He wanted to have clean boots to fly back home to Georgia that night. This had not been the best of days for Judy. She had already had to take seams out of some of Kenny's new stage clothes that had just shipped in that day. Kenny would order his stage clothes for the tours, and by the time they reached the road, the seams had to be let out. Kenny used to blame his weight gain on me! I never really believed that, but he did sign an album of mine "thanks for the extra ten pounds!" I entered the room as Kenny was heading to the stage to start his set. Judy turned and told me if I did not help her clean those boots, she was leaving for Florida the next day. When Judy said something like that, I knew she meant it. Judy and I spent the next hour cleaning the clay off his boots. What a horrible task that was!

Judy was part of my crew and traveled with us. I found Judy in St. Petersburg, and I admired her so much. I could not then and still cannot sew a straight line. Judy was a sewing machine with hands. Everyone was glad to have her on the tour. Something was always ripping, or buttons were falling off. Just do not ask her to clean your boots!

Our touring schedule enabled Kenny to keep up with the farm that he loved, his personal life with his new little son, and his other appearance schedules. Basically, our tour schedule was three weeks on, three weeks off. In those three weeks, we were in a different city every day, and we would probably have only one day off. Oh my God, a day to sleep! That was heaven for the entire crew. When we were in a motel or hotel, we slept almost the entire day and barely saw one another. There was one day off that really stands out in my mind when most of us did not sleep. We were in Texas, the weather was gorgeous, and the hotel was beautiful with a magnificent outdoor and indoor pool area. The outside area was very lush with great outdoor furniture. Just a lovely setting.

Word had come back from the truckers the night before that this place was super, so the guys asked me to make sure that I kept my blender out in anticipation of the next day. Blender in hand, we set up a magic station in my hotel room. There was lots of rum, limeade, strawberries for daiquiris, and a waste basket full of ice. The blender would whirl away, glasses were filled, and out to the pool area we all went to swim, relax, and enjoy. The outdoor area of the hotel was huge with a big sloping yard down to the pool area. It wasn't too long before the rum drinks, pool, and lovely weather had everyone extremely relaxed and tipsy. All of a sudden, one of the guys came running down the hill toward our group. Apparently, he thought that he was going into my room to refill his drink. Instead, he had gone into a different room. He could not wait to share what he had seen. His story brought everyone to attention. He had opened the screen into a room where a couple was making mad passionate love in their bed. So passionate was their lovemaking, that they did not even hear or see this strange man in their room. Being curious and a little drunk, the ten of us all ran to that same room to see if his story was true. If I had not seen it with my own eyes, I would tell you it was a fib. But it was a true story. We were all immediately afraid that we would get caught -- after we went into the room twice. Kenny would have been furious. Our drinking for the day ended with all of us going to our respective rooms. We were lucky that the police were not called. This story never got out!

Kenny had one very specific rule for the crew. We were a family show, and Kenny wanted everyone to be respectful. Absolutely no beer cans or bottles were to be seen backstage. If you were drinking a beer, you had to make sure it was in a colored plastic cup and not visible to the public. On one of our three-week runs, we had a day off in Detroit. I was planning on flying home the next day to be with my children. Whenever we had a day off, I did that instead of staying on the road and sleeping. I would fly out early, and then fly back on a red eye to rejoin the tour. This way, I at least got to see my children for the day. On that day, Kenny called me into his dressing room just before show time. He heard that I was flying home to see my kids. He told me that he was flying to Ft. Lauderdale to look at a yacht that he was thinking about buying. Kenny asked me if it would be safer and easier for me to get to my children if I flew with him to Ft. Lauderdale. I was thrilled. I told him I could rent a car at the airport and then drive up to St. Petersburg. My children were expecting me to be home when they got in from school. Now I could surprise them by making breakfast and taking them to school! I would be able to sleep while they were in classes, pick them up from school, and have the afternoon to be with them before I flew back to the tour late that same night.

Kenny was worried about my safety and kept asking me if I was sure that I would be OK. I assured him that this was a great idea. I was told to have all my gear in the limousine by the time he finished his last song on stage, because we would leave immediately for the airport. When we got to the tarmac, the pilots opened up the truck of the car. To my horror, my souvenir case of Iron City Beer with the Pittsburgh Steelers picture on the cans slide out of the limo truck and landed right at the feet of Kenny Rogers. He did bellow, "which one of you men are bringing beer onto my plane?" Not one man spoke up. Kenny mumbled, "Oh God, Midge, this is yours, isn't it?" I exclaimed that this case of beer was a prized souvenir because the Pittsburg Steelers and Terry Bradshaw had always been among my favorites. I bought the case on this leg of the tour in Pittsburgh and just had to take it home. He ordered me to pick it up and get it on the plane before anyone saw it. Kenny just stood there shaking his head as I scrambled at his feet to pick up the beer. He did not want beer -- even on his plane. As he went up the steps to get into the plane, he turned to see me taking a huge floral arrangement out of the limo. These were the very same flowers that had been in his dressing room earlier that night. He just stared at me with the look on his face of "now what?" I mumbled that the flowers were going to be a surprise gift to my babysitter, something I otherwise couldn't have gotten home if I had not been flying with him on a private plane that night. It was all I could do to get this floral arrangement onto the plane. You see, all the flowers and stuffed animals that adoring fans threw to Kenny at each show were given to me. I would rearrange the flowers the next day to use them on the crew's eating tables. All the stuffed animals went home with me to my children. I was the only one on the tour that had small children at the time, outside of Kenny's little Christopher. I always loved fresh flowers and enjoyed every bouquet, as did the crew the next day. Finally, we all were on the plane: the two pilots, Kenny, one of his assistants, and me with my beer and flowers. Kenny went to his private compartment to sleep. I curled up in one of the plane's seats to catch a nap before my drive from Ft. Lauderdale to St. Petersburg, Florida.

This was not just some ordinary plane. This plane has a story too. The plane used to belong to the President of Mexico back in the 70s. It was a Perrier BAC 111 jet with twin engines that seated 27 passengers. Kenny always traveled with two pilots. That was my first and only time flying in someone's private jet. I was impressed that I had the opportunity, much less a jet owned by Kenny Rogers. The movies are right: you pull up to the tarmac and hop on up the stairs. When the jet lands, your car picks you up at the bottom of the steps. What a thrill for this gal!

I slept all the way to Ft. Lauderdale. When we landed, one of the pilots walked me, my beer, and the huge flower arrangement to the rental car counter. I rented a car and took off for St. Petersburg planning on surprising my children for breakfast. I took the Florida Turnpike with the plans of exiting at Yeehaw Junction, cutting through Tampa and going straight to my house in Seminole. About two miles before I was to leave the turnpike, the back-left tire blew. I was mortified! What was I to do? There I was in the middle of nowhere, around 3 am, pitch black with no moon, and miles of nothing on either side of the highway. I was terrified. The stories you hear about bodies being dumped and never being found were going through my mind. The only person that knew I was on this road was Kenny Rogers – oops. I kept thinking of how Kenny repeatedly had asked if I was going to be safe. His voice was ringing in my ears. The first trucker that passed by me put on his brakes and backed up to my stranded car. I was praying big time that this person was going to be a good guy. I forgot to mention that I also had about two week's salary in cash in a money belt around my waist. As this man climbed down from his cab, I thought I was going to faint straight away. He walked up and asked me where I was going. I told him I was trying to get to St. Petersburg to make a surprise breakfast for my children. He studied me while I was saying this and then said, "Well, if you were my wife, I would hope that someone like me would stop to help you. Let's get this tire changed." One tire later, his watch was broken, and he was covered in grease. I offered to pay for his troubles, but he refused. I offered to buy him a new watch, which he also refused. All I could do was thank this kind man for helping a lady in distress. He said he would tell his wife the story. She was waiting up for him to get home with a pot of coffee and some down time before he went to bed. I was so thankful for such kindness. I was home to make breakfast for my children, which had been my goal. I never told Kenny Rogers this story.

On another date, we were in Buffalo, New York. My local runner was a delightful woman who mentioned Niagara Falls was about an hour away. I had never seen Niagara Falls, so I asked Kenny if I could run up there. This was a major break in protocol for concert tours. We always stayed together. No one took off before, during, or after a show. I begged and pleaded. Kenny asked if I trusted this woman; I told him I did. She had worked for me the year before when we had been in Buffalo. Finally, Kenny made his decision. I could go to Niagara Falls -- with the stipulation that I had to walk with him to the staging area as he went onto the stage to start his set. When he came off the stage after he was done, he had better see my "smiling face" looking back at him. I was thrilled. As he walked with his bodyguards to the round, I went running out the back door and jumped into the van with my runner and her husband. We raced up to Niagara Falls on the Canadian side. I jumped out of the van to hang over the railing. It was the most magnificent sight. The falls were gorgeous at night.

I jumped back into the van, and we raced back to the concert hall. I had been to Niagara Falls for maybe a total of ten minutes, but I had seen it. When Kenny walked off stage surrounded by his bodyguards and came into the backstage area, I was standing there with this huge smile on my face. I told Kenny that this Florida girl had finally seen Niagara Falls! Kenny had indulged me, bless his heart. It took me another 15 years before I returned to visit Niagara Falls again.

Safety of your road family was always a priority for the entire crew. Every person had a job that needed to be done, and every individual was an important part of the team to produce a show. In the 70s, most of the crews were primarily men. Very few women worked on the road. My girls and I were the exception. We were well-protected by our men. They respected the work and the hours that we put in. We worked hard to provide them with home-cooked meals. Today, there are many more women on the road crews and house crews.

One winter day, the tour bus and trucks were coming over the mountains to play a concert in the Valley of The Sun. The crew bus slipped on ice and slid off the road. We kept waiting and waiting for them to arrive for breakfast, and we knew something must have happened. No one was ever that late for the morning call. What a sickening feeling that was. Back then, we only had CBs, no cell phones. The safety back-up plan for traveling was that everyone always took the same routes. We always followed one another. My little truck, called the Chuck Wagon, would leave first so that we could get down the road while the semis were loading. The trucks and the crew bus always traveled together. Finally, after what seemed like an eternity, we watched the first truck filled with the silhouettes of many heads as it pulled into the parking lot. Then the next two trucks came rolling in. The crew bus was left in the ditch. Our truckers had picked up all the men, jammed them into their cabs, and proceeded to the venue. I was never so happy to see my guys in all my life. Everyone was fine, just shaken and way behind schedule. We all worked extra hard that day. The show went on as scheduled, and the audience never knew that a real tragedy had been averted. This was the only concert where I was told to go out and buy Kahlua and brandy for the men to add to their coffees. Everyone was bone-chilled, and their nerves were on edge, but the family was OK.

All these men were like brothers. Brothers who sometimes tormented their sisters, which was true of life on the road with some 50 men. To take a shower behind a locked door was a treat. To be able to lock the door and go naked for a few minutes was a luxury. They loved to find you, if they could. They would make you think they had stolen your clothes while you were in the shower. Sometimes, cold water would be dumped over the side while you were having a nice hot shower. The line was never totally crossed with me, because you never pissed off the cook. Tease, yes. Piss off, never.

That is not to say that I did not take part in some pranks myself. None of us were without fault. The one prank that really stands out in my mind was one played on the comic Gallagher. In my first year of traveling with Kenny, Gallagher opened the show. Every day I would buy his watermelons for his Sledge-O-Matic routine, his pie pans, and any other fruits and vegetables that he wanted for his act. There were some days when Kenny would stop the Sledge-O-Matic, because Gallagher's act would slow the show production time down. This would infuriate Gallagher. Watermelon and pieces of fruits and vegetables would get clogged in speakers and band equipment below the stage. The band and stage crews would start screaming. It was time consuming and labor intensive to clean up all this stuff up. If any of you have been to a Gallagher show, you know that there is not enough plastic in the world to cover yourself and everything around you from getting pieces of fruit everywhere. Gallagher would sulk for days when Kenny put his foot down. Sledge-O-Matic was a huge part of Gallagher's show. After a few days, Kenny would allow Sledge-O-Matic back into the show, and the entire cycle would repeat itself.

I have seen Gallagher many times since then; I consider him a friend, and I try to catch his show whenever I can. I truly love this man!

Kenny told me years later that he always knew when I was on tour. When I was there, I made sure that we celebrated every holiday. On Valentine's Day, everyone had heart candies and kiddie Valentine cards. At Easter, everyone had candy, and Easter grass was scattered all over the tables. At Thanksgiving and Christmas, the appropriate decorations abounded. Halloween was just nuts! Halloween candy and trick-or-treat bags were everywhere backstage.

Recent Reunion with Gallagher in St. Petersburg, me, Gallagher (funny as ever), and Melanie

Midge Trubey

One year, we were at LSU for Halloween. You can see by the picture that I stayed dressed all day looking goofy. Later that night, I even wore a witch's mask. All this craziness got everyone in the mood for some Halloween fun. When Kenny came into the building later in the day, he found the crew digging in road cases, making costumes to wear that night. Even the band was caught up in the spirit of Halloween. That night, when Kenny introduced his band during the show, they all stood up wearing masks. There he was on stage with his mouth hanging open and laughing. The Halloween pranks were not over yet. On that same night, the beautiful Dottie West was on tour with us (more about her later). She sang her set looking her lovely self, but when it was time for her to sing her duets with Kenny, there had been a big change in her appearance. Dottie was brought to the stage in the same way that Kenny was always ushered in. She was surrounded by bodyguards who would walk her down the aisle to the stage, but Kenny could not see her. Dottie had decided to join in on the Halloween fun by dressing up as Dolly Parton. She had powdered her gorgeous red hair and stuffed her sequined top, bosoms overflowing. Kenny was holding two microphones, one for him, and one to give to Dottie. As she took the stage, the crowd roared their approval of her Halloween costume. Kenny turned to hand her the microphone. He took one look at her and totally dropped both mikes, grabbing his knees to keep from falling over in laughter. All of us were lined up backstage to watch Kenny's reaction. He was so surprised, and his reaction was just plain hysterical. He cut their duet time down that night, because he said he could not sing love songs to her as she was so hysterically dressed. We had a blast that night. What fun!

Kenny Rogers and myself
Halloween at LSU

On the road, birthdays were always special events. I would get a birthday cake for whoever had the birthday, because they were away from their own family. Kenny and CK celebrated a little differently just between the two of them. Kenny would have me buy a cake for CK so that he could surprise CK with the cake in his face as he rounded the dressing room door on his birthday. Kenny told me that I was absolutely not to have a birthday cake for him when it was time for his own. Well, come Kenny's birthday, CK would order me to get Kenny a cake so that he could throw it at Kenny when he came into the building. I would protest, but as I told you in the beginning, Kenny and CK were both my bosses, and I was at their mercy. One year I got CK an Oscar the Grouch cake, which meant green icing everywhere. On Kenny's birthday, I got a Cookie Monster cake, which meant blue icing everywhere. Both men had beards which meant extra clean up job for themselves. After Kenny got the blue icing in his face, he bellowed, "Midge, where are you?!" I was already at his feet cleaning the icing off his boots. I had lots of hot towels handy. Each man always knew they were getting a cake in the face, but they never knew when. It was a highly-anticipated part of their annual birthday rituals.

It must be in my genes, because I have always been a big family person. I love my own family to pieces and missed them when I was on the road. With all the traveling that I did throughout the years, I would always alert my cousins and friends when I was passing through their cities. It was also a welcomed relief to see family and friends from my hometown. I missed my children so much, my heart would actually ache. One of my dear cousins, Jim, and his wife, Debbie, lived in Little Rock, Arkansas. They were far away from their parents and family, same as me, and Debbie was pregnant with their first child. I wanted to see her so badly, and bless her heart, she came out to the Cow Palace (yes, I said Cow Palace) to sit and visit with me while I cooked. I did not realize just how pregnant she was! Plus, that day was just bitter cold. I took one look at her and was terrified that she would get sick or catch something from all the wind blowing under the doors. Lots of stuff was blowing around. I found a stool for her to sit on by my stove to keep her warm, grabbed some blankets, and wrapped her up. We had a wonderful visit. She and I still laugh about that day so many years ago. She looked like a little pumpkin all bundled up! It was visits like this that made my long days so extra special.

I had cousins come to visit after they got off from work. Other cousins would help me shop for specialty items and give me a hand for the day. Sara Jane, a cousin in San Antonio, would bring Texas BBQ as a treat for my crew. She was only about 4 feet 10 inches, but she knew how to hustle. She would have the restaurant load up her pickup truck with this fantastic BBQ and barrel to wherever I was cooking that day. The men would always help unload her truck.

As with any large concert, there were opening acts. I have already told you about Gallagher, a true wit and comic genius. Many of the other opening acts became my good friends. Each of them also had contract riders that included their particular wants for their dressing rooms. Of all of these fascinating people, two ladies were at the top of my favorites list: Crystal Gayle and Dottie West. Both women would rotate into the tour, but never at the same time. Both were country music power houses during these years.

You already know that Dottie West had a terrific sense of humor from my previous story. I just loved Dottie. I never saw her with a frown on her pretty face and never heard her say one bad word about anyone. She was just a delight, a lovely and gracious lady. The music world lost a great voice way to soon; Dottie has been gone for many years now. She was gorgeous on stage and a delight backstage. When she performed, her red hair shinning, her vibrant personality glowing, and her glitzy stage clothes sparkling, no one was better. One of her songs I remember most is Country Sunshine. Dottie would finish her set, leave the stage, then Kenny would come on. She would come back during the show to sing duets with Kenny. Their big song at the time was Every Time Two Fools Collide. Dottie was always gracious and would leave me little notes saying how much she and her band appreciated our cooking on the road. As our days were long, these little notes meant so very much. I still have one of them, written on a cocktail napkin, that I cherish. She was married to Byron Metcalf, her drummer, in the late 70s. He was just the nicest guy and a great chili cooker. Byron's recipe for chili is still one of my favorites! He wrote the recipe for me on some hotel letter head, which is one

Me and the gorgeous Dottie West in 1980 with one of the notes from the dressing room that I saved from her

of my prized possessions. Byron was handsome, and Dottie was gorgeous. They were a great-looking couple. Before my time working for Kenny was finished, Dottie and Byron divorced. The fast pace of the music world is known for breaking up many couples. It is sad to say, but they were a prime example of that world taking its toll.

I have mentioned before that we traveled as one big family on the road, with all trucks and tour buses following the same route. We would follow each other in case of any break downs. We had CBs, but again, communication while traveling on the road was tough. One particular night on the way to Cincinnati for the filming of the Kenny Rogers' Americana television special, our RV broke down. Dottie's tour bus, The Sunshine Express, plucked us off the highway. If Dottie had not stopped for us, we would have been late for crew call on a very important date. This was the same night as Dottie's birthday, and her tour bus was rocking! All the Personal Touch crew wanted to do was sleep, because our breakfast call was extra early because of the filming. But that night on The Sunshine Express, the most important thing was Dottie's birthday. Everyone was still whooping and hollering when The Personal Touch crew was dropped off at the Cincinnati stadium. We tumbled out of the tour bus, with no sleep, to greet a back-breaking workday. The group on the Sunshine Express checked into the hotel for a day of sleep.

Kenny's television special was a huge production, "Kenny Rogers Americana." Not only was it at a huge set up at a stadium, but we had all the extra television crews to feed. I was especially excited, because one of my best girlfriends, Nancy, was coming to visit me. I had not seen her in years. We had had no sleep at all, so I instructed my crew to take a nap; I would do breakfast by myself with Nancy helping me get set up. As the guys started coming in for breakfast, my stamina finally gave out, and I literally could not stand any longer. I was exhausted. My dear girlfriend, a mother of six children, really knew her way around the kitchen, but was about to do more at this breakfast than she had bargained for. I asked her, begged her, to cook eggs on request for my crew so that I could take a short nap. Nancy was scared, but God bless her, she jumped right in. When I got up, Nancy was still at the stove cooking, frying, and scrambling eggs, looking as natural at the stove as she had looked in our Home Economics classes back in junior high. They loved her. She really saved me on that tough day! What a mess that could have been! We still laugh about it today.

When Crystal Gayle appeared on the Kenny Rogers tour, I was thrilled. Her voice is like a soft breeze with birds singing. Her husband, Bill, travels everywhere with her. Both of them are just so nice. Their down to earth attitude and joy for the career that they have chosen is very apparent. Crystal is the entertainer, Bill handles all of Crystal's legal affairs. They had no children at the time. They were always laughing and enjoying the tour. Each day they entered the venue with big smiles on their faces. Aside from her beautiful voice, Crystal is known for her very long hair that sways when she sings. When she takes her shoes off, I have seen her hair dragging on the floor behind her as she walks around her dressing room. As the tour progressed, I was usually the first person to arrive at the building to set up breakfast for the crews. I would sometimes pick out the dressing rooms for the advance. Only one time did I not choose a room for Crystal that she did not like. It is funny that I remember that, but I do.

To this day, I love going to see Crystal and Bill wherever she is singing. I have seen her in Orlando for a corporate convention at the Marriott. She requested that I cook for her in the backstage area. What a shock it was for me when the head chef showed up backstage to meet the woman that had replaced him for the evening! I have been to a mountain fair ground in North Georgia, to Ocala, Clearwater, Pinellas Park and St. Petersburg, Florida on several occasions to hear this lovely lady. I went to Nashville, Tennessee to sit front row when she was inducted into the Grand Ole Opry at the Ryman Auditorium. Her sister, Loretta Lynn, did the presentation. What a night to remember sitting with my friend, Cyndy, watching the magic of Loretta Lynn, her sister, Crystal, and her sister, Peggy Sue, singing together on the same stage. Iconic to say the least!! Throughout the years, I have gotten to know Crystal and Bill's two children and many more of their family members. Life is amazing. All these years, Crystal and Bill have always welcomed me and my family with open arms. Now that I am retired, traveling to various cities to visit with my friends, instead of working is a true joy.

The beautful Crystal Gayle 1981

This would be a good time to give you an example of the food rotations that I used on tours even the tours that were done only in the state of Florida. I have mentioned to you that the crews were manly men, hungry men.

Breakfast to start the day: Orange juice and any other requested juices, Milk, Coffee, Cream, Sugar, Sugar substitute, Assorted cereals, English muffins/bagels, assorted breads, butter, cream cheese, assorted jellies and jams, peanut butter, assorted yogurts, hard boiled eggs plus eggs cooked to order, Gatorade, bottled water, fresh fruit, hot tea, honey, lemon slices, and assorted sodas. These items were to be available

The glamorous back stage life photo courtesy of The South Bend Tribune

until lunch was ready to be traded out. The beverages were to be available all day always.

Lunches were very important. Deli trays can get so very boring pretty quickly even with supplying different breads and rolls but some of the men, just loved making their own dagwood sandwiches. What is not to love about that? But lunch rotations included:

- Deli trays with cheeses and various breads and rolls
- Hot dogs and hamburger
- Make your own taco bar
- Sloppy Joes
- Grilled cheese and tomato soup
- Tuna fish salad, egg salad, vegetable soup
- Sliced tomatoes, lettuce, pickle assortments, various side salads (at least a choice of two daily), always fresh fruit (seasonal and regional whenever possible), fresh bananas, various chips, cookies or brownies, candy bar assortment

Chips, candies, fruit, and cookies were always left out for the entire afternoon for munchies.

Dinner for a large crowd of men was actually easier than lunches. We always rotated, New York Strip roast, Baked ham, Baked pork loins, meat loaf, beef Tenderloin, and steaks on the grill, and baked fish. These were in addition to the recipes that I am sharing with you in each chapter. Seafood was always popular in Florida and lobsters were always a hit in Maine. With the baked ham, we served scalloped potatoes. Pork loins were always served with freshly made applesauce, my creation and mashed potatoes. The comfort foods always reigned supreme, as lasagna, beef stew and on occasion, baked chicken (sometimes, the guys would say "fowl", maybe they meant "foul". Tee hee) Tenderloin and steaks always had baked potatoes with all the toppings. Mixed green salad with the choice of various dressings was always served, believe it or not, even back then, the guys always loved their salads. Fresh vegetables were always preferred. If not fresh, frozen vegetables seasoned could be served but never canned vegetables unless they were the Le Sueur peas. Dinner desserts were rotated too, assorted pies, cakes, anything that might look extra good at the bakery that I visited daily. Strawberry short cake with whipped cream and banana pudding was popular. I could bake cookies on the road but there was never enough time to bake enough cake or various pies for the head count that I was feeding. I had to rely on the store bakeries. Rolls and butter were a must at each meal.

Comfort food, a home styled cooked meal, is what I offered. I wanted the men to think they were raiding "Mom's" refrigerator and cabinets at home. That was my goal. I think that most of the time, I accomplished that goal.

I look back on my "Kenny Rogers" years as some of the best years of my career. I have a personally signed copy of his new Memoirs, Luck or Something Like It. He was been a big supporter of me writing my book. He told me he wanted a signed copy of my book as "I know the author". I said "Holy Cow" to that one! I just wish I could have carried out his request.

In all my Kenny Rogers stories, I would be totally remiss if I did not mention some of the wonderful people we worked with behind the scenes. Many were with him until the end of his career. This speaks volumes not only of Kenny, but for the whole crew working together all those years. I have already mentioned CK Spurlock, who was the promoter during those days. Ken Kragen was his manager at the time. You felt Ken's presence as soon as he walked into the room. He was tall with striking red hair. He never asked for anything that was not already in the dressing room. He was polite, but always watching. Those of us that traveled together showed loyalty and commitment to The Boss; we loved our jobs. These people were the backbone of any show. During my era, my Road Brothers were Garth, Lelan, Paul, Tim, Lanny, Keith, and Gene.

From the Nashville office, Debbie handled the special requests concerts on the road. Folks, that was a lot of paperwork and coordinating as we did not have computers then! She was the nice voice I always heard at the other end of the telephone telling me what needed to be done. Not too many years ago, I called the office to tell Debbie that I wanted to go to a specific show. I wanted to bring the guys food, so I asked Debbie to find out if they had any special requests. Debbie called back laughing with their answer: "She knows us well enough to answer that question herself." That reply, after all these years, made me feel great and right back at home. I never asked again; I just cooked or baked and went to the concert to see my friends. Many times, I loaded Kenny, the band, and crew busses with food for their all-night drives.

To be successful, an entertainer must have a good band, and Kenny had one. These guys had been with him for many years. When I was first on the road, I was the one with little children. I have watched this band get married and have their own children. When you have known people for a long time, the nicest visits are getting caught up on our kids' lives. The age of computers made it so much easier to keep up with pictures of the wives, families, and children. My days of having to remember which band member liked peanut M&Ms versus plain have passed, but we have a ball seeing each other and visiting. When we all were traveling together, there was just no time to visit. Life moved so quickly; we were always running from one place to another. I was glad that these talented men stopped for a few minutes to reminisce with me. It was always a great night to see these friends; I miss these visits.

Life changed for Kenny Rogers in his later years. He was still on the road making the great music that millions of people still loved, just not as many dates and not as many large venues. Until I retired, I would cater for him whenever he was in Florida. Kenny married his current wife, Wanda, during that time. I was able to meet her before they got married. I had Gene hand carry a wedding present back to Georgia. The next time he was in Florida after the wedding, Wanda sought me out backstage to thank me for their present. I became a huge Wanda fan. Kenny was now the one with little children; everyone else's were grown. Kenny and Wanda have these adorable twin boys that kept everyone on their toes when they came out on the road. Backstage for little children is a world of wonder and excitement. I know this because I raised mine backstage. Now it was Kenny's turn.

Most people don't know that Kenny was a photographer. If you have never seen his photography, you are missing some of the most gorgeous pictures ever taken. In 2010, Kenny released a calendar of some of his photos. In it, he wrote, "One of the benefits of my job as an entertainer is that I am constantly traveling the world with phenomenal beauty all around me." Truer words were never spoken. When you are on the road, you see touches of life and beauty, and you hope you can return someday to really enjoy the sights and sounds instead of rushing through it. I am so glad that he shared his photography work with the rest of us. He wanted to show his twins the world that he loved so much while he could.

Not too many people can hold an audience in the palm of their hand night after night, but Kenny Rogers did. Whether it was a small, intimate concert hall, a Christmas show, or an MGM concert for thousands, the man had charisma on stage that set a high standard for anyone in the music business. He wanted to show his twins the world that he loved so much while he could and made sure they were with him on tour as much as possible.

All of us that had him in our lives are struggling with his passing; he had such a profound effect on all of us. I think he would be surprised at how much we all miss him. I still cry, but then I can laugh about so many wonderful memories. I miss him and my road family greatly.

One more Kenny-ism. He would say "This leg of the tour, I need to diet, so Midge, I only want fish or chicken as my entree. What's for dessert? I'll take two."

Kenny Rogers is still one of the most beloved entertainers in the music world. He entertained us for over 60 years. To this day, I still call him "My Boss" and a cherished friend. His passing March 20, 2020 left a huge hole in my heart. Kenny Rogers' will be forever missed.

I will always love you, my friend. Thank you so much for always encouraging me.

Ray Decker, my husband, Kenny Rogers, and me.

Me, Melanie, Kenny Rogers and son in law, Phillip, Christmas Concert, St. Petersburg, Courtesy of Randy Dorman Photography

Baked Fish

This recipe is so easy and so good. I like to use cod, haddock or grouper, nice thick pieces. Buy for how many people you are going to serve, I figure about ½ lb. per person, remember, I am cooking for hungry men.

◇◇

Place the filet on aluminum foil in you baking dish. Put a nice coat of mayonnaise on the fish, I use Hellman's or Dukes, not Miracle Whip. Sprinkle sliced black olives on the top of the fish along with paprika for color. Cut a scallions and sprinkle both onion and green stems on top of your fish. Then, place pats of butter along with top of your fish, at good intervals whereas the butter melts, it will lightly melt over the top of your fish. Bake at 350 degrees until your fish is done. If you like lemon with your fish, squeeze some fresh lemon juice on the top as you take it out of the oven. This is just yummy with wild rice, with a colorful vegetable on the side. Easy and good, everyone will wonder what the nice sauce is on top of your fish!!!

When I put "baked grouper" on the menu board for dinner, the men ALWAYS changed the wording to read "baked groupie", I know you will not do that!

◇◇

Midge Trubey

Mayonnaise Parmesan-Crusted Chicken Breast

Quick, so easy, and keeps the chicken breast moist.

◇◇◇

1 c Hellman's mayonnaise

1 c grated Parmesan cheese

4 boneless skinless chicken breast halves, pounded to about ¼-inch thickness for even cooking

◇◇◇

Combine 4 tsp of seasoned dried breadcrumbs plus another 4 teaspoons of grated Parmesan cheese

Preheat oven to 425°. Combine Hellman's mayonnaise and ½ cup grated Parmesan cheese in a mixing bowl until well blended. Arrange chicken breast on your baking dish (I line baking dish with foil for easy clean up). Spread mayonnaise mixture evenly over chicken breasts then sprinkle with breadcrumbs and cheese mixture.

Baked for approximately 20 minutes or until chicken is thoroughly cooked.

Baked Corn Souffle

Double this recipe if cooking for 6-8 people,
everyone will want seconds.

◇◇◇

1 can creamed corn

1 can whole kernel corn, undrained

8 oz sour cream

1 stick butter, melted

1 box Jiffy corn muffin mix

1 egg

◇◇◇

Mix all the ingredients together and pour into a 1½ quart lightly greased baking dish. Cook at 350° for about an hour.

Midge Trubey

Byron's Chili Recipe From The Road

Thanks to Byron Metcalf for this great recipe.

"Byron's Chili" for 60

22 lbs	Very Lean Ground Chuck or round	
80 oz	Tomatoe Sauce	
10	med Onions - chopped	(8)
7	minced garlic cloves or equivilant of dehydrated chips	
10·T	Cayenne pepper	(5)
10·T	chopped Jalapeño peppers	(5)
10·TB	Oregeno	(5)
12·TB	Cumin	(6)
40 Rounded TB	Chili powder	(20)
10·TB	Paprika	
10·T	Salt	
12·TB	Masa Corn Flour (very Important)	
20	Regular Size Cans Plain Pinto Beans	
6	small cans Old El Paso chopped Green chiles	(3)

garlic Salt, Salt + Pepper

→ #9. Heat Beans w/ salt to taste

10. Add Beans + Stir just before serving   serve w/ crackers & milk

HOLLYWOOD-COUNTRY CLUB FLORIDA

1. Lightly brown meat with onions & garlic

2. add tomatoe Sauce + equiv. of water

3. Add all ingrediants except Jalapeño + flour + beans

4. stir at light boil or simmer 1½ hours.

5. AFTER 45 min. TASTE For Hortness + Add Jalapeño a little at a time (every 5 min or so) till just Right!

6. Skim grease

7. mix flour w/ warm water till barely thick (Almost Runny) + add slowly to thicken.

Holiday Inn | 14800 HOLLYWOOD BOULEVARD HOLLYWOOD, FLORIDA 33026 PHONE 305/431-8800

8. Simmer 30 more min. + Stir

Handwritten recipe "Byron's Chili" from 1980, Courtesy of Byron Metcalf, Percussionist and Shaman

Kenny's Special Peach Chicken

I was given this recipe by Marianne so many years ago.
I put my own spin on it, and Kenny still loved it!

— Serves 6 —

3 boneless chicken breasts, split	Brown sugar to taste	1 c of flour
		Salt to sprinkle
Large can of peaches with syrup or fresh peaches	Touch of cinnamon to taste	1 tbsp of butter and 1 tbsp of margarine
	2 eggs, beaten	

Split your chicken breasts to 6 halves. Pound them between saran wrap (same as you did for chicken piccata in Sam Moore's chapter.) Melt both butters in your skillet. Dip each breast into the egg and coat with flour. Sprinkle each breast with salt as you are cooking, each breast about 5 minutes per side. Make sure you do not burn flour in your skillet, add more butter if need be. In a separate bowl, drain your peaches (when using canned) saving your peach syrup. In a separate saucepan, melt a little butter, place drained peaches in pan with brown sugar and cinnamon to fit your taste buds. Cook the peaches down to where they are slightly colored. As you chicken breast come out of their skillet, place chicken breast in your baking dish. Take your peach syrup and lightly pour over your chicken, enough for taste but do not put so much peach juice that your chicken breast is swimming. Too much juice will make your breasts soggy. Then place a peach half on each breast, put into a 350° oven for about 20 minutes, or until heated through out. Serve with rice.

If you use fresh peaches, put peeled peaches into saucepan, add brown sugar and cinnamon and some peach brandy to get your sauce going, you can add a little orange juice also. Just make enough juice to put on top of your chicken cooked chicken breasts. Then put your fresh peaches on each chicken breast and into the oven, same as above.

You just want to heat enough for the chicken breast to absorb some the peach juices and bring back up to temperature.

Midge's Famous Lasagna Recipe

I just had to say that to tease you. My lasagna has been requested by Kenny Rogers, Crystal Gayle, Billy Joel, and Donna Summer to name a few. The crews looked forward to me making it, even to the present day. I have made this recipe for my children and their friends forever. It is always exciting for me when I make it, as adults now, they always share their fond memories, making me feel so good! This is one recipe that I will not share with you. I will make it for you anytime, but this is one recipe that I will keep to myself.

Growing up Roadie

One Thanksgiving, the band, Heart, was playing in Jacksonville. I told the promoter that since it was a long weekend, I did not want to leave my children home. The crew of Heart was the best. I worked with them many times and knew it was a safe place to have my children backstage. The promoter checked with the band, and I got the OK to bring the children. I called my Mom and asked her to move up Thanksgiving dinner so that we could be at her house but still get to the show in Jacksonville. I told my children that we were taking a Thanksgiving road trip. My son, very seriously, informed me that since it was a holiday, we could not leave his basset hound, Rosie, at home. She had to come with us. I made another call to the promoter to check, and the message came back, "Just get to Jacksonville, all is OK." So, my son and his dog, along with Heart's dog and dog sitter, walked the circular Jacksonville Colosseum. It has since been blown up. As the concert time approached, there was my daughter, Melanie, sitting on a road case next to the stage watching from a secured area. And there was my son, Corbett, sleeping on his mattress beside my stove with his dog. Rock children and dogs can sleep through it all. As it was a long weekend, I had planned an extra treat for all of us. On our way back home, we stopped at Sea World for the day and night before heading back St. Petersburg for school on Monday.

Backstage was always an extremely secure place. My crew and children wore the Kelly-green shirts that identified us, and we became well known. We also had security badges to show that we were allowed in our areas. Other people were to stay out. One particular show in Tampa was a repeat for me. The show was wonderful. I had taken Corbett with me for the day, and we were going home immediately after the show. He followed me around all day doing his thing. Right before any show, the backstage mood became electric with the final light and sound checks, people getting dressed, and dressing room checks. I turned around and could not find my son. I ran to check all his favorite places, but no Corbett. I went everywhere backstage, and still no Corbett. I called the show security; they had not seen him for about 10 minutes. We called the local police, who were already in the building. I was panicked beyond all belief. The police told me he could not have gotten far, and they fanned out in the concert hall. I was almost hysterical. A few minutes later, the police captain came to me and said they had spotted Corbett. They

Monday

Lunch - 1-3:00
Deli Tray
Asst. breads
Mayo/mustard
Potato salad
Cole slaw
Chips
Fresh Fruit
Egg salad/Tuna for vegies
Lettuce/Tomatoes/onions/pickles
Cookies

Dinner
N.Y. Strips on The grill
Baked potato c̄ sour cream; bacon
Fresh brocolli
Tossed salad c̄ choice of dressings
Fresh strawberry shortcake
Rolls with butter

Vegies: Tortellini

A sample of one of my daily notes to the crew

Midge Trubey

had not approached him as they did not want to scare him. There was my son, in the audience, intently watching the show and swinging his little legs from the seat. I retrieved him and brought him back to our secured area. I asked him what he was doing because he knew he was not supposed to leave the backstage area. He answered very logically. "Well, mother, we have worked all day, and everyone said that the start of the show is wonderful with the fireworks and lighting. I did not want to miss what everyone had been talking about all day." This was the only time that he got away from me.

My daughter has always been beside me throughout my business journeys. On many an occasion, when I did not want to travel for a certain show, she would insist that we go together. She wanted to see her favorite bands. My Melanie loved her music, and she kept current with the entertainers that she loved. To keep her busy during her days off of school, I would let her bring one of her girlfriends along to help wash dishes, set the tables for meals, and lug ice from the ice machines. The reward for being a good helper would be to sit backstage at a great location and watch the show. This one particular show, Adam Ant and the Romantics, I noticed that Melanie and her friend Rory had left to change out of their Kelly-green t-shirts into more presentable clothes. They emerged in tight jeans and bejeweled t-shirts, and their hair was spray painted and spiked in a thousand different colors and directions. I had a total hissy fit, taking them back into the kitchen area and putting their heads under the faucet. The girls were howling so loud that it brought the bands out of their dressing rooms to see what was going on. My daughter and Rory informed me that they had never been so embarrassed in their entire lives and proceeded to call the other girl's mother to come pick them up. They were so mad at me that they did not want to stay for the show anymore. I did not want my little girl to look too grown up backstage at show time, no way, no how. I think she was 14 at the time. Melanie and I tell this story a little differently as time has passed, but this is how I felt as a mom.

My two children and I used to have family meetings to discuss our upcoming schedules what was expected of each of us. My job was to provide money for our house and to put food on the table. Their job was to do well in school and help Mommy around the house. If the three of us worked together, we would have lots of time to play. We would make lists of local places that we wanted to go, like the beach, the park, Busch Gardens, Sea World, and of course, Disney World. We all knew that we had to work together; We were the Three Musketeers. If I had to travel without them, I called them every day. Calling home in those days was challenging to say the least. Cell phones did not exist, and there were only pay phones backstage. They had their schedules, and I had mine. Sometimes we just could not connect. We missed each other terribly. When I was home, I joined all the school field trips, and

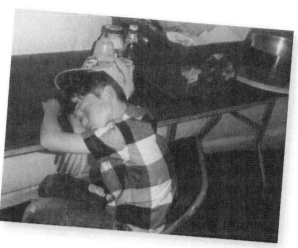

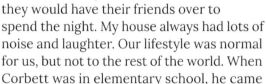

A young Corbett, exhausted from hanging out backstage with Mom.

they would have their friends over to spend the night. My house always had lots of noise and laughter. Our lifestyle was normal for us, but not to the rest of the world. When Corbett was in elementary school, he came home from school crying saying he would never go to school on a Monday again for the rest of his life. He was miserable. He told me his school friends thought he was a liar when he stood up in front of the class to show and tell about his weekend adventures with his family. I immediately picked up the telephone to call his teacher. I will be forever grateful to him. What he explained to me made perfect sense. He explained that on Mondays, children would stand in front of their classmates and talk about their weekends. There would be stories about camping, days at the beach, going to Disney, and spending the night with the grandparents. Then my little boy would stand up and tell the class he had met Michael Jackson in Lakeland for his show. Or he would tell the class he had seen a show with lots of fireworks inside a concert hall. The children would laugh at him and think he was lying. They could not remotely imagine what my son had seen. The teacher told me that even though our life was normal for us, it certainly was not normal for the average American family. My children, to this day, say they had an unconventional, normal upbringing. I loved them more than anything. I had them before my business, but my business was the only way I had to make money to support us. I knew that I could not stay on the road forever. I missed my children way too much, and they were growing up without me.

Melinda's Breakfast Casserole

I pull this recipe out when it's my turn to fix Christmas brunch eggs.

Serves 6-8

6 eggs, well beaten

4 c of whole milk

1 tsp salt

¼ tsp pepper

1 small onion diced

½ tsp dry mustard

2 c croutons, flavored or plain

1 c sharp cheddar cheese, shredded

6 slices bacon, cooked dry and crisp, then crumbled or 1 c diced ham, or 1 c cooked and crumbled sausage or 1 c sliced mushrooms

Spread croutons in bottom of a buttered 13×9 baking pan. Sprinkle with shredded cheese and diced onions. Combine eggs, milk, salt, pepper, and mustard, mix well and pour over croutons. (Croutons will rise to the top) Sprinkle with bacon crumbles or whatever you have decided to use. Bake at 325° for one hour or until firm. Test by inserting knife in the middle of your dish, done when comes out clean. Let sit for 15 minutes before you serve. (For Christmas morning, I have everything prepared and keep separate until I assemble in the morning while the coffee is dripping.)

Melanie's grits breakfast casserole

Catching on to what my family loves? We love Sunday brunches! This is one of my daughter's favorites.

Serves 6-8

6 c chicken broth	2 c regular grits	4 large eggs, beaten
1 tsp salt	16 oz. cheddar cheese, cubed	½ c (1 stick) unsalted butter
¼ tsp pepper	½ c milk	
¼ tsp garlic powder		8 oz grated sharp white cheddar

Preheat the oven to 350°. Grease a 4-quart casserole dish.

Cook 1 lb of breakfast sausage (you could also use bacon or ham and then dice) in a frying pan, drain and pat the excess grease and moisture from the sausage then set to the side.

Bring the broth, salt, pepper, and garlic powder to a boil in a 2-quart saucepan. Stir in grits and whisk until completely combined. Reduce the heat to low and simmer until the grits are thick, about 8to 10 minutes. Add the cubed cheddar and milk and stir. Gradually stir in the eggs and butter, stirring until all are combined. Blend in the cooked sausage (or other meat) then pour the mixture into the prepared casserole dish. Sprinkle with the white cheddar and bake for 35 to 40 minutes or until middle is set.

Midge Trubey

Ray's Big Apple

We use my Mom's 10" cast iron skillet. Have your New England Maple syrup ready! Delicious!

– Serves (oops, this feeds just Ray and I) –

Preheat this skillet for 5 minutes in the oven at 475°, take out when you are ready to assemble your "big apple".

Sauté 1 ½ c sliced apples in butter, use another skillet, not the one mentioned above.

In your blender, blend:

◇◇

1 c flour	6 eggs	½ tsp salt
1 c whole milk	1 tsp vanilla	¼ tsp nutmeg

◇◇

Blend and scrape the sides down, blend again

In your hot skillet from the oven, melt 2 tbsp of butter at the bottom of the pan, coat the entire bottom of the pan

Add your apples to the buttered cast iron skillet, make sure they are evenly spread out

Pour the batter on top of the apples in the cast iron skillet

Bake at 475° for 15 minutes then reduce your heat to 375° for 10 minutes longer.

Aunt Betty Jane's Chicken Liver Pate

A family must-have that we always begged my aunt to bring to all our family celebrations.

1 - 8 oz package of chicken liver, thawed and drained

¼ c chopped onion

¼ c chopped celery

4 tbsp margarine

¾ c chicken broth

¼ tsp paprika

¼ tsp salt

Dash of pepper

1 clove garlic, minced

2 tbsp brandy

1 tbsp unflavored gelatin

2 hardboiled eggs

In skillet cook liver, onion, celery, and garlic in margarine till livers are brown and vegetables tender. Add ¼ cup chicken broth and seasonings. Simmer covered for 5 minutes. Remove from heat, stir in brandy. In small pan, soften gelatin in remaining broth and heat to dissolve. Blend liver mixture at medium speed with hand mixer. Place in bowl and add gelatin. Chill till beginning to set. Add chopped egg white and yolk from one egg. Pour into a 3-cup mold. Refrigerate until set. When ready to use, unmold, spread with 1/3 cup mayo mixed with 1 teaspoon mustard. Chop remaining egg and sprinkle on top. Serve with crackers.

Fresh Sweet Potato Au Gratin

I picked this recipe up in the mountains in my little town of Blue Ridge, Georgia. I love it!

— Serves 6-8 —

1 tbsp butter, softened

4 medium sweet potatoes, peeled

and sliced thin

2 tbsp light brown sugar

2 tbsp marmalade

2 c heavy cream, must be heavy cream

Butter a 9x13 baking dish. Layer the potatoes into the pan in rows. Mix together the brown sugar, orange marmalade and cream, I use a whisk. Pour over the potatoes. Bake at 350° oven covered for one hour. Remove the cover and cook another thirty minutes until the cream is thickened and a golden brown.

Noodle Kugel

One of my dearest Jewish friends was appalled as she said this recipe was better than hers!

– Serves 15 –

½ lb wide noodles

½ c (1 stick) butter, melted

1 c sugar

1 - 8 oz carton cottage cheese

½ pt sour cream

1 - 4 oz package cream cheese

4 eggs, room temperature

1 - 8 oz can crushed pineapple, drained

1 c golden raisins (soaked for a couple of hours in water until plump, then drain well)

3 tbsp marmalade or apricot preserves

Cinnamon and sugar to sprinkle on the top

Cook noodles in boiling water about 10 minutes, rinse with warm water, add melted butter and toss to coat evenly. Place in buttered 9x13 baking dish (light grease this baking dish before you put your noodles in). In a blender put sugar, cottage cheese, sour cream, cream cheese and eggs, blend well. Add this to the noodle mixture. In a separate little bowl, mix the pineapple, raisins, and marmalade. Add this to the top of your baking dish. With your spatula, lightly part your noodles so that two mixtures blend in with the noodles in your dish, just mix slightly. Sprinkle sugar and cinnamon on the top of your dish (sometimes, I do not add this sugar and cinnamon depending what I am serving this with, whether a side dish or as a dessert)

Bake at 350° for about one hour, top should be golden and bubbly. Remove from oven, sit up for about 30 minutes before serving. I like to serve this warm. If you want to serve cold, refrigerate covered and then cut into squares.

Midge Trubey

Dishing Up Spring Break

When I look back on the Spring Break concerts I worked, all I can say is "wow." I don't know how I handled the workload. I must give credit to my legions of employees who helped pull it off for so many years. The situations were just crazy!

From around 1980 through 1988, the Personal Touch worked with MTV for their Spring Break concerts. I was responsible for feeding film crews from MTV and Campus Network Television along with all the staff producing the concerts, all the headliners for the shows, local police departments directly involved with our security, plus VIP hospitality food areas for the sponsors of these shows. If you watched any of the MTV or Campus Network productions beach concerts on television, I can guarantee you that I was there along with my trusted sidekicks. These events took us to Daytona Beach, Ft. Lauderdale, Pensacola, Panama City, and Ft. Walton Beaches, Florida.

Typical stage set up for Spring Break Concerts, Daytona Beach

The shows were live from the beach cities, broadcast from right on the beach. Daytona Beach quickly became the main site for the majority of the concerts. Ft. Lauderdale decided pretty early on that the spring breakers had worn out their welcome. If you have never been involved with a spring break event, all I can do is shake my head... Our sponsors included Budweiser, Miller, and Hawaiian Tropic. Hawaiian Tropic was in its developmental years at the beginning of the 80s, and as I look back, what a smart business move that was for them. Hawaiian Tropic is a household name when it comes to the beach. Budweiser and Miller have always been the drink of choice for college students all over the country, whether parents want to admit it or not.

The local Florida promoters involved year after year included Albert Promotions, Fantasma Productions, along with excellent local

Growing up Roadie

companies, such as Jack Link and Associates, that handled stage, lighting, and sound. Every March, we all became this dysfunctional family working on the Florida beaches to make Spring Break successful.

Every March, I loaded up the refrigerator truck and moved to Daytona Beach. One year, after the refrigerator truck was loaded on my way out of town, I went to say goodbye to my parents. I can still see the look on my dad and my mom's faces when this rumbling truck pulled up to their house. My dad was shocked to see his daughter jumping out of it; so much for southern charm school! I think they were relieved to see this big, noisy truck roll away from the front of my childhood home.

In Daytona, I rented a huge barbeque grill and an ice box loaded with ice. Whoever was making the local arrangements for the concerts procured tables, chairs, and tents for the feeding areas. The artists were given RVs for dressing rooms since the stages were built right on the beach. A VIP tent was usually provided near the side of the stage for special guests of the sponsors. This tent was also furnished with tables and chairs. In Daytona Beach, the famous band shell was the background for the huge stage that was built in front of this unique facility, and it always looked fabulous on television. As different promoters and sponsors were involved with these productions, it was the local guys that made sure there was continuity for these shows so that once the basic area was set up, it stayed that way for the entire break.

The huge stage in Daytona Beach was built out in front of the existing band shell. The existing stage was nowhere large enough for these television shows. The band shell was directly on the beach, which made it convenient for all the college students. As it was on the beach, bathing suits were the attire of choice. In front of the big stage, there was a secure area of about 6-8 feet to keep the crowd from jumping on stage. Security guards were always in this area to protect the staff and entertainers. There was no backstage, only a few very small rooms in this historical building that were used for production staff. There was no air conditioning either. The make-shift backstage area was the RVs parked in a large semi-circle in back of the building around the food tent. This arrangement helped create an area that gave some privacy for the crew and entertainers. The entertainers had air-conditioned motor homes without much area for food, so most of the entertainers ate right alongside the crews. This created a huge beach-party atmosphere backstage. Beyond this area, the band shell had its own security wall which helped our security men keep the beach goers out. Unfortunately for me, there was not enough room for my refrigerator truck in the closed off area. The local police and our security teams would protect me going back and forth to the truck. In all those years, I never had an issue with safety or security as I was running back and forth.

Speaking of back and forth... Since Daytona Beach became my home base each year, my children loved the Fridays. I had the same hotel for years, and teenagers were not allowed to check in. As soon as my children got out of school for the week, they were brought to stay with me in Daytona Beach for the weekend. On Sunday, they went back to St. Petersburg for school the next day. When they had their own spring break, they would stay with me the entire time.

I started letting my son Corbett come to Daytona Beach when he was in kindergarten. Corbett was an old backstage hand by then. He knew he had to stay within the secure area, and the police and guards were always watching him. As we had these different sponsors, one day, he would be a walking billboard for Budweiser, and the next day he would be dressed in Miller gear. He wore his bathing suit or shorts along with the appropriate t-shirt of the day, beach cap, sunglasses, and carrying the appropriate cup of the day for his sodas. He had a special place on the coquina wall that sloped just enough for a him to crawl up on, relax, and watch the comings and goings of the backstage area. I knew I could find him in his spot or out in front of the stage just watching. Corbett had freedom in a secure area that most children could only dream about. Except for the one time he disappeared in Tampa and about gave me a heart attack, Corbett was my little buddy always sharing with me his adventures. I never had any complaints about him being backstage with me from the promoters, entertainers, or their staff. Many of the entertainers took him under their wings, and he would visit them when he made his rounds each day. I am thankful that I had such a great relationship with the working crews that allowed Corbett to be there.

My daughter, Melanie, was in middle school, a preteen who knew what shorts she needed to bring, how her hair would look, and made sure that the t-shirt of the day was tied just so. She was just darling and of course, her mom made sure that everyone backstage knew from the get-go that this beautiful girl belonged to me, and she was not some stray girl in the backstage area. That girl was a pleasure to have around, and she would help me with anything that I needed. She knew to stay in the backstage area; the crowds were so huge that she could have easily disappeared. That thought always scared me. She loved the beach scene, plus all her school mates would go crazy hearing her stories each Monday morning at school. Melanie has always been the child with a smile on her face and a song in her heart. I am a totally blessed woman when it comes to my children, then and now.

When our workdays were over, back to the hotel the three of us would go. The swimming pool was the highlight of our day.

A typical workday on the beach started with the breakfast call from 7 am until approximately 9 am. This would mean that I had to be on site around 5:30 am each morning. The beaches on March mornings were usually freezing, with bone-chilling air coming off of the Atlantic. Sweatshirts and sweatpants were a requirement for those early-morning hours. By the end of breakfast, my crews were in their shorts, company t-shirts, and sunglasses slathered in Hawaiian Tropic suntan lotion. The Personal Touch t-shirts were highly-recognizable; if you had a Personal Touch shirt on, no one questioned you moving around all the RVs and the other secured areas. We got all the promotional t-shirts from the spring break shows, but we never wore them on show days. My son, Corbett, still wears some of my saved t-shirts as collectors' items.

Melanie with one of her teen heart throbs, lead singer of Mister Mister, back stage at Daytona Beach

Our biggest concern was having plenty of beverages and ice for those hot days. Instead of having canned sodas, we arranged for the local distributor to provide soda machines. Juices, Gatorade and jugs of water were a necessity. In those days, spring water was mostly in gallon jugs, so lots of cups were needed. Come 9 am, breakfast snacks had to be left out so anyone could grab something to eat at any time. From 11 am to 1 pm, Lee was king of the grill. Lee traveled so much with me; if he was not on the grill, it was me. Hamburgers and hot dogs were grilled to order, no sitting in the chafing dish was allowed. All the fixings were provided with lots of salad choices and fresh fruit. Some days, we would have BBQ chicken on the grill, and

Midge Trubey

145

another day might be steaks; it would depend how many days we were working with the same band. A big hit was always a cake in the shape of a beer can, Budweiser or Miller, whichever was sponsoring the day. Cookies and candy bars were very popular in the afternoon. Due to the live television broadcasts, most of the show times were during the day. By show time, all the RVs, stage areas, production rooms, and VIP areas all had to be stocked.

The concerts were awesome and a sight to see with thousands of screaming, bathing-suit clad college students pushing towards the stage and dancing in the sand. I had a ball watching the show from the on-stage area. Watching the audience was just as entertaining to watch as the musical acts. Every once in a while, the stagehands would encourage the girls in the front rows with signs saying "show us your tits," and the girls would gladly flash in response. It was one big party atmosphere in the audience, on stage, and backstage as well. Everyone was happy for the most part. It was spring, the weather was fabulous, and we were having one big picnic. My crew was delighted to have the daytime concerts, because we could get back to the hotel way before sundown and have some time to relax and regroup. There would be an occasional night concert, which was tough on us. I was concerned with the lighting in the RV area since security was tougher at night. It was harder to see if anyone was trying to sneak in, and the local police were always worried about the large groups. At night, the college crowd was better off in a night club or walking on the strip where they could be seen. It was always a tragedy to hear that someone had fallen over a balcony due to heavy drinking. Regular public service announcements were broadcast from the stage asking everyone to drink responsibly.

Working in Daytona Beach was the Cadillac of the spring break shows. We had a physical building, the backstage area was paved, and it had better security. In Ft. Lauderdale, Panama Beach, Ft. Walton Beach, and Pensacola Beach, the stages were built directly on the sand. Everything was in the sand! The Florida panhandle cities are known for their white, silky sand, but by the end of the day, I hated that gorgeous sand. Everything was in the sand, and the sand was everywhere. Running from RV to RV and to and from the grills all day was exhausting. Sand got in all the equipment and covered our bodies. By the end of those show days, I felt like I had been in a giant sandbox all day.

As the Spring Break concert years wore on, the atmosphere felt like a dysfunctional family reunion with the Florida road and production crews, along with the local workers. All of us looked forward to seeing each other year after year. Not only were these shows good money and good business, but we also knew that we could rely on each other to produce the best show possible for the visiting artists and camera crews. It was important to each of us to provide the best experience we could to all the companies and individuals. I remember all these men became my brothers every March for approximately eight years.

The schedules were packed. My 1984 Spring Break included:

- March 14: Big Country at the Daytona Beach Band Shell
- March 14: Aldo Nova at the Plaza Hotel, Daytona Beach
- March 15: REM at the Daytona Beach Band Shell
- March 15: The Fixx and Modern English at the Plaza Hotel, Daytona Beach
- March 16: Blue Oyster Cult with Aldo Nova, Jacksonville Coliseum (not a spring break production)
- March 18: Blue Oyster Cult with Aldo Nova, Lake Civic Center (not a spring break production)
- March 19: The Fixx and Modern English, Ft. Lauderdale
- March 20: Mike and Dean, Ft. Lauderdale
- March 21: Heart, Ft. Lauderdale
- March 22: Heart, Daytona Beach Band Shell
- March 24: Kool & the Gang with the Dazz Band, Daytona Beach Band Shell
- March 25: Duran Duran, Jacksonville Coliseum (not a spring break production)
- April 21: Heart, Ft. Walton Beach

As you can see, there was a lot of traveling up and down the Florida coast. These were regular concert dates needing breakfast, lunch, dinner, dressing room set ups, and load outs, so I did all these with the refrig-

The ever loyal, Lee Leland, manning the grill in Ft Lauderdale, Florida

Midge Trubey

147

erator truck and my road-case range. I would cook at the back of the truck in Lakeland and Jacksonville. Then, back to the beach schedule with breakfast, lunch, RV set ups, and a hospitality tent. Crazy as the schedule was, I still had my usual family time in Daytona with my children.

My babysitters drove the children over to Daytona for Heart's March 22nd show. Those gals and their crew were always so nice to work with. I remember asking Ann Wilson to sign an album for my ex-husband; he had always been a big Heart fan. I recall her laughing as to how would I like her to sign it. She said she'd never been asked to sign something for an ex. She asked if I wanted her to write "F*** you" and then sign her name! I told her no, it was all good. We had a good chuckle over that one. I have a great picture of my son, all decked out as Budweiser Man, with Ann. It is one of my favorite pictures of those spring break years.

Back when I first started my business, Barracuda was at the top of the charts. My son was about two, my daughter was almost eight, and for whatever reason, the two of them loved this song. As I mentioned, their dad was a big Heart fan. When he played this song, the children would instantly turn into maniacs, running around the house, arms waving over their heads, jumping off the couch, and jumping three stairs up from the landing into the family room. All the time, they would be singing, "Barracuda!" Melanie was old enough to keep her balance, but Corbett would run around after his sister, falling all over the place. When she jumped off the couch, he would do the same, always hitting his head or toppling over as small children do. He would pick himself up, laughing all the time, and continue to run after his sister. Wherever I was in the house and heard this song start, I would drop whatever I was doing to run watch the children in hopes of keeping my baby from killing himself. I told Ann about Corbett's dancing, and she told me that when they on stage ready to sing this song, I should get Corbett to the secure area in front of the stage. On cue, I grabbed my son and got him to the front. There on MTV, Ann dedicated the song to the young man standing in front of the stage – my Corbett! I was so excited for my son. Well, the event was not a happy one for him. With his hands on his hips, this eight-year-old looked up to me and said, "Mother, you always embarrass me," and he stomped off to the backstage area. So much for that special moment! To this day, whenever I hear Barracuda, I think of my little children running, singing, laughing and jumping throughout the house.

During the spring of 1984, Duran Duran was making their appearance in Jacksonville. My Melanie was one of the millions of young

Dishing Up Spring Break

Ann Wilson of Heart and Corbett before concert in Daytona Beach, 1984

teens that could not get enough of this band. One of the band members had family in Clearwater, Florida, and sightings of him brought a frenzy with these teenage girls running all over in hopes of running into him and his friends. Thank goodness Melanie was not driving at the time, or she would have been part of that crowd. Duran Duran was to these young teens what the Beatles were to me and my sisters growing up. As Melanie got older, she got more vocal about what shows she wanted help with so she could see her favorite acts. When she heard that I was going to cater Duran Duran, she almost passed out, insisting that she had to come with me, or she would die. She talked me into skipping school for that date. She was a great student, so it was a no brainer for me. Corbett went back to St. Petersburg with the sitter, and Melanie went with me and the crew on to the Jacksonville show. Thank goodness I was able to go back home after that concert, daughter with me, after a grueling schedule. I had a few weeks to get the sand out of everything before heading up to Ft. Walton Beach to work with Heart again.

There are so many more stories from my 8 years of working spring break concerts. Calvert DeForest was one of the neatest people. Not only was he super nice, but what a comic! The college kids loved him. No words were needed; when he walked on stage, the crowd would go crazy clapping and screaming. He had this winning smile, and boy, did he make great facial expressions! My children loved him, and he would talk with them and was genuinely glad to see them. Whenever they weren't there, he always asked about them. If the name Calvert DeForest isn't familiar to you, how about the name Larry "Bud" Melman? They are one in the same person. Ring a bell now?

I was thrilled to meet Billy Crystal. He was on all the TV channels with his famous "you Look marvelous" phrase. Before the crowd was let into the auditorium, I had my children sitting in the front row; there weren't reserved seats. Bill came out into the auditorium with Calvert to check out the house set up. Both men stopped to talk with my kids while I was backstage finishing up their dressing room set ups. Melanie got him to say "you look marvelous" to her. She still

Midge Trubey

149

smiles to this day whenever she sees a clip of him saying his famous phrase.

When Jan and Dean performed at the Daytona Beach band shell, everyone knew we were watching history in the making. Dean rarely traveled, and it was very special to have him in Florida, on the beach no less. It was very draining, and he needed assistance to get on and off the stage. We all watched him to make sure he did not trip and were so happy to see "the legend of the song." He loved singing the set, and what fortitude this man possessed. I am sure Jan misses him today as Dean has passed away.

Melanie dancing on stage at concert Daytona Beach, Mike Love insiste

It was not uncommon for me to be given a schedule of events, only to arrive and find several more dates had been added at God knows where. The Personal Touch traveled with the entertainers, promoters, and sponsors, providing our own brand of catering and making a homey atmosphere wherever we went. I received a last-minute call to cater for Starship in Daytona Beach and Pensacola Beach. When Melanie heard that I was potentially going to turn down the Pensacola Beach job, she insisted that we all go together to the other side of the state. I informed her and Corbett that road trips in a refrigerator truck were no picnic, to say the least. The truck sat two adults in the front, and the suspension was not the best. Corbett, from his sister's prodding, said that it would be a great adventure. "Come on, mom. Let's do it!" My sister had in laws that lived in Pensacola, so I asked them to be my work crew there. My regular crew would not travel so they could stay in Daytona Beach to be fresh for the two following shows. What an experience this was!

Behind the wheel of the refrigerator truck with my children in the cab traveling from Daytona Beach to Panama City

Going to Pensacola Beach from Daytona Beach was a long, bouncy drive. I had had a good night's sleep the night before, so I was rested.

Pensacola was sandy fun. Melanie and Corbett worked extra hard to help me, and I had the long drive back to Daytona Beach after the show. This was after working on the beach since 6 am, working in the sand until about 6 pm, and packing up to leave. Absolutely no sleep or rest for me at all. I made arrangements with a hotel closer to the concert so the children did not have to come with me so early the next morning for breakfast setup. I figured they could sleep in and stay locked in their room until I came to get them after breakfast. It sounded logical. Well, it did not work out that way. I was driving in the middle of the night with my two children sleeping on top of each other in the seat next to me. As we bounced back to Daytona Beach, I really had a hard time staying awake, realizing I let myself be talked into doing something that was not necessarily safe for my family. It was a lesson that I would not repeat again.

When we finally arrived in Daytona Beach, I drove to the hotel to claim the room that I had paid for in full two days prior. I was shocked when the attendant told me that they had already rented out my room since it was 4 am and figured I was not coming. I reminded him I had already paid for the room to make sure it would be available for us; he couldn't have cared less. I had two children that needed to go to bed, and I needed at least a couple hours sleep before I had to get started with breakfast for the Jan and Dean concert. The children were still sleeping in the truck as I climbed back up into the cab and drove across the street to the Band Shell.

The area was on full security lock down as the RVs were in place with all the backstage equipment. I found the security guard who, thank God, recognized me right away. I told him what had happened and asked him for the keys to one of the RVs. Having anyone at all in the RVs was a huge no-no. I begged and pleaded for the keys, which he eventually gave me. This dear man guarded the RV so the three of us could sleep. I carried my children into the RV, and we stretched out and fell into a deep sleep. He woke us at 6 am so I could get breakfast going. Melanie and Corbett were so tired, they did not hear the knock on the door about 1 ½ hours later. I thanked the security guard for his kindness. Both of us were well-aware that we broke the rules of no one being allowed to sleep in the RV. As I fixed breakfast, we both kept an eye out for the show's manager to show up. I caught sight of him just as he got to the door of the RV where my children were sleeping. I called to him, running in his direction. I retold the story of our hotel room disappearing, and he was aware I had been in Pensacola Beach the day before. He was understanding of my dilemma but was not happy about the kids sleeping in the RV. I promised him that nothing was damaged nor dirtied, and I would wake the children before anyone from the band arrived. About 10 am, I woke them. Our hotel story spread throughout the day. Jan asked Melanie to dance on stage with them that afternoon during the concert ; it was customary for the bands to ask some of the cutest girls in the front rows to join them during the last number. I think Jan felt it was a reward for being such a good sport. Corbett couldn't have cared less. He was on his perch on the coquina

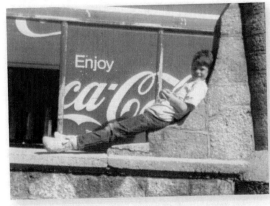

Corbett's favorite spot back stage at Daytona Beach. Perfect spot for a young man to see everything going on in a secured, protected area.

wall, watching everyone come and go. When the concert was over, I had never been so glad to see my bed that night in my regular hotel. That was one long couple of days.

After having a day to rest and go swimming, it was time for the Beach Boys in concert – on the beach. How perfect is that? The men were still talking about my driving experience from Pensacola. Mike always let me watch the show from behind the speaker, sitting stage right. I was, and still am, a huge Beach Boys fan. When it came time for him to call the girls to the stage, Mike walked over to the speaker and pulled me up on my feet to join in. I was the first woman dancing. You should have heard the hooting and hollering from the crew when they saw "mom" dancing up on stage! That was the only time I danced on stage; the experience was a total blast.

1987 brought some changes to the beach. Bill Graham Presents from California was hired to change the face of the spring break productions. He was a very famous promoter primarily in California. His "Days on the Green" concert events were phenomenal. They were huge events at the Oakland Football Stadium where top-named bands would play huge concerts that lasted all day. Mr. Graham's backstage areas were all about the bands and their comfort. It included carpeted ground, plants, tables with umbrellas, tablecloths, and ambiance of a more elegant picnic area. Ron, from Bill Graham Presents, was in charge of the Daytona Beach shows that year. The backstage area was transformed into a California-type look. The game had been upped!

I was fortunate to be able to work with Bill Graham concerts when I was on national tour with Journey in the late 70s. Journey was one of the bands playing in Oakland where Bill Graham Presents produced his Day on The Green. The look of the backstage area, as I previously described, was ahead of its time. Mr. Graham set the bar.

In March 1987, the concerts were fast and furious. All the sponsors were present, along with MTV and Campus Network. There were days that I knew I was catering, but had no idea who the acts were until they came backstage. Some of them included my friend Eddie Money, Bruce Hornsby and the Range, Limited Warranty, Crowded House, 'Til Tuesday, and KC and The Sunshine Band. Most of my notes say breakfast from 6:30 am until 9 for 50-75 people, lunch from 11:30 am until 1:30 for 100-150 people, and dressing room #1 and #2. The VIP area was to be set by 1 pm. The days came and went in a flurry.

Years later, Bill Graham was helicoptering from one concert to another. His helicopter crashed, killing him. I was very sad. When you are on top in this crazy business, you cannot move fast enough to get from one place to another. Many an accident resulted from the fast-paced atmosphere. Lynyrd Skynyrd was a legendary crash. There have been other bus crashes that have probably been forgotten. Gloria Estefan was hurt in such a crash. Touring is a dangerous business that the average person does not even realize. Those of us that have worked all day and driven all night have been lucky to stay alive, but some have not been so lucky. One such lovely man was Rocky, the production manager for Dimensions Unlimited out of Washington, D.C. Rocky had worked a show all day and was driving to the next day's concert by himself. We think he fell asleep behind the wheel, killing him in a crash, leaving behind a darling little daughter. I remember crying for days over the loss of this man. The lesson that all of us on the road tend to forget, is faster is not always better. You have to be safe at all times while doing your work.

As I take a hard look at those Spring Break years, I have such mixed emotions, both business-related and personal memories. Business-wise, each March, I knew I would be working on a beach somewhere making steady money. I would see my children on weekends. My work clothes consisted of sweatshirts in the morning as the beach would be so cold before sunrise. When the sun came up, t-shirts, shorts, and good running shoes was all that would be needed, along with a good sunscreen like Hawaiian Tropic. Most days when the afternoon concert was over, I could go to the hotel and fall into the swimming pool before collapsing into bed, the next day would begin with the same schedule, different bands. When we had night concerts, which were not the norm, the days were extra-long and the local crews and bands looked forward to steaks on the grill. By the end of the day, sand was everywhere. Cleaning, cleaning, cleaning was a must to keep everything sanitary for all of us workers. After spring break back in St. Petersburg, I would be cleaning equipment for days; sand, sand, sand everywhere. You could never have enough ice on show days, so the iceman became my best friend. A smile went a long way, and last-minute requests were the norm. "Oh, Midge, can you get this?" or "Oh, Midge, we forgot that" or "Oh, Midge we need to add this for tomorrow." This meant running somehow, some way to the grocery store which meant less time in my hotel swimming pool, something I really looked forward to. I kept smiling as I knew taking care of these requests fed into the big picture of a successful event. Spring Break Shows were a big deal back then. My friends and family would watch the shows on television all over the country to see where I was and with whom I was working. For me, the beach was a big deal in itself. I was born in Florida and brought up as a beach baby. Nothing is better than a day at the beach, and this childhood memories never leave you. Memories of running, running and more running. I always knew I would get great exercise in March. When the beach workdays would get crazy, all you had to do was look out into the crowd, the speakers, the lights, and see that gorgeous beach. Aaahhh, life can't get any better than that view! The gorgeous beaches of Florida hold many a great memory to the huge population of beach lovers all over the world.

Me and my children, Daytona Beach, typical of us from 1980-1988

Pat Trubey's Broccoli Salad

A different side dish for a picnic.

— Serves 10-12 —

2 packages of frozen chopped broccoli	1 c sliced green pimento olives	Salt and pepper to taste
1 c chopped celery	3 chopped hard-boiled eggs	Hellman's mayo or Dukes to your taste

Run hot over the frozen broccoli until all frost I gone, drain very well and pat dry. Put broccoli into the refrigerator until it is cool. Mix all the remainder ingredients together and chill. Best if chilled for a couple of hours before serving. Only use enough mayo to blend your salad together.

Midge Trubey

Midge's Potato Salad For A Crowd

My attempt at duplicating my mom's potato salad which always was, and will always be, the best I have ever eaten. My mom never wrote it down.

— Serves 10-12 —

5 lb bag of red bliss potatoes

1 medium sweet onion, chopped in small cubes

3 stalks of celery, sliced

Pickle juice from dill pickles

8 hardboiled eggs, cubed

2 tbsp of mustard

Hellman's mayonnaise or Dukes

Salt and pepper to taste

Do not peel potatoes, cube and cook in salted water until done. Strain immediately, put hot potatoes into mixing bowl and pour about ¼ cup of pickle juice over potatoes. While potatoes are hot, they will soak up the pickle juice. When potatoes are cooked, drain off any excess pickle juice. Add chopped onion, sliced celery, chopped hard boiled eggs and mustard. Next add enough mayo to gently coat your potatoes to bind ingredients together. I personally love mayonnaise but too much will make your salad runny, so just coat enough to hold your mixture together. You can always add more later after it has been chilled in the refrigerator. Add salt and pepper to taste. Potato salad is always best after it has been chilled for at least 3 -4 hours or overnight. When you take your bowl back out of the refrigerator, stir your potato salad. Potatoes will soak up the mayonnaise, you might want to add a little more for a creamy consistency.

Reinvention

Leaving the Kenny Rogers National Tour, was a life changing decision, that affected me both emotionally and financially. Later in life I would look back on this decision and see how pivotal it was, but in the moment the bills were coming in so I had to come up with a backup plan pretty quickly. Before I created my company, I always felt that I was a mom first. Back in the day, cell phones didn't exist, so the only way I had to connect with my children when I was not home was the use of a pay phone in the backstage area. Answering machines did not exist either, so I could not even leave a message for them. Days could easily pass without being able to talk with my children. They had their schedules consisting of school, after-school activities, and just playing with their friends. As a mom, frustration was building. I cried a lot missing them, especially on Mother's Day, a sacred day for all moms. One year when I saw our winter touring schedule with Kenny, I knew I had to make a decision. That particular leg of the tour started December 26th on the other side of the country. For me, this meant that I had to truck west on December 21. I was not willing to leave my children for Christmas; it was just not an option for me. At this point, Melanie was not even a teenager, and Corbett was just starting kindergarten. I loved my job, but I loved my children more.

I had a lengthy talk with Lelan Rogers, Kenny's brother, about my dilemma with the schedule. Leland asked me to reconsider. You did not have the luxury of picking and choosing when you were going to show up for work. It was all or nothing. Lelan wanted to make sure I understood what I was doing, so I slept on this decision for one more night, as he suggested. I reconfirmed my decision to leave the tour the following morning. I just could not handle the long touring schedules anymore. I was leaving my great road family to be with my own family.

Well, home I stayed. My children were happy that Mommy was not going to be gone for long periods of time. Mommy was a little frantic about making ends meet, but I immediately called all the Florida promoters to tell them I was not going out on long national tours anymore. I asked them all to put me back on their local schedules for groups coming through Florida. I was so lucky; I was welcomed back with open arms. I had a good reputation and work ethic. The bands and groups that I had worked for when I first started out were very happy to see me back in the regular touring circuit. I was happy to

Midge Trubey

see them too. My children were happy to have me back home. I went on school field trips. We went to the beaches and played in the parks. I was home, loving every minute of being a mom.

When the Florida shows came up, I still had my babysitters in place to help me with the children. My workdays were still terribly long, but I came home late at night after the concerts and fixed breakfast for my own children in the next morning before I took them to school. Once they were at school, I collapsed for some much-needed sleep. Life was good, and the bills were getting paid, because I lived within my little budget.

It wasn't long before the Florida promoters and the bands themselves started to offer me more opportunities for work. I was always interested in making money. I had to be; I was now a single parent raising two little children by myself. Spring Break, the month of March became a tradition with MTV and College Campus Network Television from 1980 to 1988. I was hired as the rehearsal caterer for the Michael Jackson Victory Tour in Birmingham Alabama in 1984. Short road stints with Molly Hatchet, Prince, the Beach Boys and the O'Jays followed. "Short" is the key word here.

Running my own company afforded me the opportunity to take my children backstage with me when I knew they were safe in a wholesome environment. Most weekends, found my children with me at a concert. This was still not an ideal situation to fit into a school schedule and them having their own friends and a "normal" upbringing. My son was teased in the 4th grade when, during Show-N-Tell, he told the class that he had spent the weekend at a Michael Jackson concert. His school friends thought he was making the story up, very difficult for a young child. As his teacher told me, "Not the norm for a 4th grader." What was normal for us was not the typical family normal. Big decision time for me. I had to move away from the concert business.

I secured a commercial kitchen and went after a catering license to produce parties, weddings, and events here in my hometown. I had to beg people to hire me in the beginning. Everyone assumed that since I cooked for all these wealthy entertainers, I would be too expensive to hire for a daughter's wedding, or the dinner party they were having in their home. My answer was always, "Let me give you a quote and help with ideas to make your party fantastic."

Slowly but surely, the word spread in my community that I was available to handle catered functions. I realized very early on that most hosts were panicked to throw parties, plus weddings were sheer terror. I loved putting these events together! I had much more time here at home than when I was on the road. When you have a party, you need flowers. I found myself working with other florists until I figured out it would be easier if I was my own florist in charge of my own flowers and decorating. That was an instant hit! When I consulted with a potential client, I was able to provide their food, theme, and flowers, all accomplished at one interview. Next came the site inspections for flower placement and food presentations. I found out that most people needed to rent tables, chairs, and linens, so I did that too. I would soon provide any item that my clients needed to take stress off of them so they could relax and have a good time at their own party. I thought it was terrible for a host to spend money on an event and not have a great time. It made no sense to me. Ease and fun for the client was always my approach. My business was getting bigger.

At this time, I had my catering company, my flower shop, and I was still doing some Florida concert tours for my most favorite people. Now, I was lucky enough to be able to pick and choose. I was busy in my community, my children were happy, and I was back to volunteering for local organizations, too.

Then the Super Bowl came to Tampa in 1984. The Super Bowl then was very different from the Super Bowls of today. In the 80s, each client (Ford, Chrysler, Chevrolet, etc.) was able to hire their own caterers from an approved list from the host city without major control of the NFL. Each caterer would be bidding and advising each client on what could be done and what was available for their tent in the tent village. You could be very creative. Today, the NFL controls every aspect of the tent village parties.

At that time, my professional kitchen was at one location, and my work office was at home so that I could be in the house when the children came home from school. They would have their friends over, and again, life was good.

I got my name on the Super Bowl Task Force list for approved caterers. In those days, only local caterers were used. Later, the phone rang, and it was a large travel company representing Chrysler Corporation. One year out from Super Bowl Game Day, I was supplying tents, bands, port-o-lets, power, signage, tables, chairs, linens, site locations, decorations, and food for Chrysler Dodge and Chrysler Plymouth divisions involving 750 people. The ideas that I presented were a huge hit with Chrysler and the travel house. I called a very good friend of mine, Debbie, to assist putting this entire project together. Thank goodness for her!

So much is involved when you are working for clients, as I have described, whether big or small. Attention to details is essential in all phases. The first important part of this Super Bowl was the selection of the site locations for the tents on Super Bowl Sunday. The tents were located that year in Horizon Park, adjacent to the stadium. As I drove around looking at the various sites, I noticed dips in the ground, plus I was looking for ease of the buses bringing in the clients for the day, plus ease for the clients to walk to the stadium. I walked from all the sites to the stadium recording how long of a walk the clients would have. Being a Florida girl and knowing our weather, I stayed away from low-lying areas in case of rain. I submitted my site plan with tent locations and positioning to the City of Tampa, and I got their stamped approval.

By the end of August, plans were in full swing, and we began to tighten down all the arrangements that I had been making for all those many months. I drove to Tampa to re-check out the tent sites. To my utter horror, the City of Tampa had decided to beautify the park by planting lots of trees. The problem for me was that they had planted them in the middle of my tent locations! I had my signed and stamped location approval from months ago in my hand. After several meetings with me fighting with the City, the trees were begrudgingly removed. Word reached Chrysler what had happened, and I was known as "the woman who moves trees for us."

My tromping around the park months earlier paid off too as it rained for several days before the Super Bowl that year. My chosen sites were high and dry, while the others were under water. I learned it is always too early to celebrate; the night before, a city water line burst underneath one of our tents. Debbie and I were taking turns with site construction. My poor friend go so sick that night after re-constructing one of the tents, come Super Bowl Sunday, she was too sick to get out of bed. Months of work, and she never saw the completed project.

After Super Bowl XVIII, for which we received rave reviews, I was hired to handle Super Bowl Sundays around the country from 1984-1988

My sister, Alice, at my first Chrysler Super Bowl in Tampa, Florida, 1984

Reinvention

for the Chrysler Corporation. All aspects of Super Bowl Sunday were my specialty from the time the buses left the hotel until the buses took the clients back at the end of the evening. These giant parties each took an entire year of planning, and several site inspection trips were needed. The beauty of this schedule for me and my little family was that I knew each January I was going to be in a Super Bowl City. I was paid a lot of money that afforded me the opportunity to invest in buying a home and commercial property for my businesses. I invested in myself for the future. When I needed to make site inspections during the year, I was able to set these trips up around my local business and my children's schedules. That was glorious! In each city, I had to interview caterers, florists, decorators, rental companies, security, city officials, and Super Bowl heads. Electric and bathroom facilities for the sites, and placement of all items, had to be detailed. The key word here is detail, detail, detail. The earlier I could secure my site and all the details the year before, the better it was for my client as they got first choice of all of the above. These giant contracts eased me up financially to better provide for my family. The month of January in Florida was not a big concert or catering month, which made it easy for me to be out of town. After each Super Bowl, I always planned a special vacation with my children when I got back home. One year we went to the Bahamas.

Working Super Bowls for Chrysler has given me so many memories, mostly fantastic! I met some fascinating people, like Mr. Lee Iacocca, the leader of Chrysler in those days, along with so many of his wonderful department heads and vice presidents. A huge thrill for me was talking with Carroll Shelby of Shelby Cobra fame. He was a friend of Mr. Iacocca's. Just dynamic. Our talk centered around chili. He asked if he could use my stove and a pot to cook his famous chili. As he cooked, we talked. He told me he had a line of chili-making boxes coming out soon which he was very proud of. I asked what made his chili

Me serving beverage to Mr. Iaccoca, Palo Alto, Super Bowl, 1985 so special; he told me it was adding masa. Sure enough, to this day, I love finding and buying his two types of chili in the grocery store. One is a traditional, regular chili, and the other one is a white chili. His ingredient of masa is clearly marked on the box. You can add so many things to this recipe to make it your own. Carroll Shelby was a nice man of many talents.

The same incentive company that I worked with for Super Bowl opened more doors for me on several other huge functions. Good performance pays off. In 1985, I was the site coordinator for a huge contract for Coca Cola Foods here in the Florida, which took over one year of planning. In 1986, the 100th Birthday of the Statute of Liberty in New York Harbor found me involved in yacht catering with fireworks displays for five yachts for two days. That was a tremendous thrill. The logistics of transporting all the equipment, staffing, and the bulk of the food from Florida to New York was a nightmare. That was difficult for all my staff. Of course, I took my children with me. They watched the fireworks from the balcony of the hotel in the city while I was on a yacht in the Harbor.

To this day, I keep in touch with the logistics coordinator from all those years ago. Barbara and I still shake our heads on how many projects and events we put together. Some were doozies! One of them was a huge convention in Orlando that involved a helicopter dropping flowers in a swimming pool at a resort as marching bands led the clients into the party area, followed by a professional alligator show.

The work on these big events was grueling, but ever so rewarding. Not only from a creative point of view, but monetarily as well. I still live in the house I bought all those years ago, the one that my children grew up in with their friends. By selling the commercial properties I invested in, I was able to retire when I was 59.

As the company grew in stature, more interesting projects presented themselves for me to undertake. My rock and roll catering started it all. Then came regular catering, the flower shop, then corporate parties and events around the country. At the end of the 80s, my city did not have too many places for people to hold their weddings and receptions. This was before the boom of hotels with banquet rooms for private parties. I started looking for a place that could be my own banquet hall, and I found it in 1990. I named my place Mansion By the Bay, and I owned and operated this facility until I retired in 2007.

Between 1989 and 2007, my company ran school lunch programs in day-care centers in our county. A day care center called me out of the blue and asked if I would do their lunch program. The children at their school were throwing away the lunches from their current company. This was unacceptable for these school owners, because in some cases, lunch was the only full meal these children got all day. I loved little children, so I got into my car and went to the school for an interview. When I saw all these preschool children, I was hooked. Little did I know, but I was soon to find out you cannot just go in and cook at these facilities. You must be licensed, approved, and inspected by the State of Florida. The rules and regulations are completely different from regular catering requirements. Well, this was a success too. This one little school led to many daycares which led to school lunch programs at private schools and two different college campuses in Pinellas County. Each private school had their own requests and requirements. The day care centers were all on one menu that was approved far in advance with the school and the state of Florida. I never would have dreamed that I would be the School Lunch Lady at so many schools.

I was running 6 different kitchens for 7 different operations. On the whole, these operations were successful. But there was one program that I had high hopes for that just did not make it. I did not own the facility; I tried for three years to make it work but finally closed that operation in 1993. I just could not make it work for me, nor my staff, nor my clients. I could not allow one department to bring all the other operations down. Each department had its own business rhythm, and together they could help one another. If one became a drain to the others, I had to change direction or cut it loose. The company was like riding a wild bucking bronco, each day different, with a different set of challenges and solutions. If an idea did not work out, I had to be willing to make changes in direction to keep the company rolling. My employees and clients relied on me continually to move forward. I always tried to be fair to both staff and clients.

I look back now, and I never could have accomplished all these operations and locations without so much help from my dedicated staff

My wonderful staff surprised me on many occasions, sign on main street of my office

and family. My sisters worked, as did their children, and then their children's friends through high school and college. My sister Alice worked from day one of my company until I retired. She was on my first contract and still on the payroll when I closed. My staff was amazing, a true bunch of dedicated workers. Our work hours were crazy, but my staff believed in me. In 2002, I even married the love of my life, Ray. I give him credit for taking me on. The poor man never knew what I was going to do next with my business. Working with a spouse can be less than ideal, especially when the business runs a seven-day work week. Egos must be put aside as well as jealousies. For the business to survive, the client must always be number one. Balancing business and your personal life is a juggle. Somehow, Ray and I made it through.

My sweet children will always be my children, but they have their own careers and homes now. They both say they had the most conventional unconventional growing up. I took them with me whenever I could when I worked out of town. I had definite rules concerning their grades, plus house rules when we were home. We really had some great times together. I just feel badly for all those times that I could not be home with them; they were so exceptional. They both understand that I did what I did to provide a living for myself and for them. I did the best that I could.

My son, Corbett, and his husband live in Los Angeles, both accomplished professionals in their fields (not any of the businesses I had!). Their home is a haven when I get the chance to go visit them. Corbett loves all types of music to this day and has a creative mind that just does not quit. His writing ability, along with his creativity, is so much fun to hear about. He even has an Addy award to his credit for his writing in advertising. He loves to travel and is very good about planning trips. I miss him every day, but my heart sings with his happiness and joy for life.

My daughter, Melanie, is the sweetest girl that ever drew a breath. She tried several times to break away from the business, but always came back. I believe she felt like she had to watch over me. She was always at my side, right up until my retirement. When my retirement plans fell into place, I asked her if she wanted to run even one of the companies for herself. She said that she was not being offensive, but she was not willing to give as much of her time as I had. I understood exactly what she was saying. She was more than ready to have her own life, marriage, and decent hours to spend with her husband. I am in awe of this woman, her abilities in the business world in which she works, her kindness to everyone, and her love of life.

I enjoy seeing my children as adults. I love being with them. The Three Musketeers grew up in different directions but together. I am so thankful.

When I retired, I had all these dreams of traveling and visiting all the sights that I had always wanted to see but never had the time with my work schedule. I also wanted to write this book. I bought a cabin in the North Georgia mountains as a family retreat and was ready for retirement of 6 months in Florida and 6 months in the mountains. However, my life has always been different from what I thought it would be.

My husband was not ready to retire. He got very involved with volunteer work that held meaning to him. Every person has their right to be happy in what they do, and Ray made his choice to plan all trips around his volunteer work. I had loved my 6 months schedule, but it came to a screeching halt when Ray took ill. I could not stay in the mountains while my husband was having health issues. So, we kept the cabin, but I came home to find a "new me." I knew I had to find something new to do with myself while my husband continued on with his volunteer work. Shopping was not for me; I had shopped my entire business career. Lunch with the girl friends was nice, but my mind was not into that.

Well, along came an opportunity by sheer luck. I ran into one of my ex-employees. She had a job working for the Tampa Bay Rays Baseball Team and loved it. You only worked when the team was in town during the season, and you had flexibility with the days that you worked. Oh, my, I was excited. This was the only job interview that I had since I was 22. I was scared to death! I was so pleased that I was offered a job to work in the box office for our national baseball team. It was so normal! I had a job in my own town and didn't have to leave. I grew up loving baseball as St. Petersburg has always been a baseball city.

At this stage of my life, working for baseball team has been one of the best experiences for me. I am not a manager; I work on a box office team with a wonderful woman in charge. I like being part of the team without all the responsibility that goes with running a department and crew. The people that I work with come from all walks of life, and they all have so many stories. I love hearing every one of them. We are all ages; I am the second oldest on the crew. We work hard together and enjoy being part of one of the best baseball teams in the league. Yes, I am very pro Rays. There are times when I work in the phone room helping clients by answering the phones "Tampa Bay Rays, this is Midge. How can I help you?" On many occasions, I get asked, "Are you Melanie's mom?" or "Midge Trubey, is that you?" When I am working the ticket windows, I see many of my old customers. They always ask, "what are you doing here?" My answer is "I am having a ball doing something completely different." I am so thankful to the Rays for giving me such a great opportunity.

My wonderful team of workers pushed me to get this book published, this book that I had written many years ago. They told me that I encourage them all the time to create and reach their own goals, and enjoy it. They told me I was forgetting my own advice. I am forever grateful for my new work buddies encouragement. Rays Up!

Where retirement is going to take me next, who knows. I am ready for what life is going to bring in these changing COVID times. The pandemic of 2020 has changed the way we work, think, shop, and live. Reinvention is going to be the name of the game for many people and industries. The possibilities are, indeed, endless. Scary and exciting all at the same time! Our changing business climate is a great opportunity to for the younger generation to create new jobs and new opportunities. Look around, be creative!

Ready for the Tampa Bay Rays Baseball Team to win The World Series

Reinvention

Ray's Coconut Fried Shrimp

This is so, so delicious!

– Serves 4-6 people –

2 lbs large shrimp, uncooked, peeled, deveined with tails on	4 ½ c coconut, shredded	1 tsp coconut extract
	½ tsp baking powder	16 oz sweet marmalade
3 c all-purpose flour	2 c water	1 ½ oz Grand Marnier liqueur

Prepare batter by sifting 2 cups of the flour and baking powder together. Add ½ cup of the coconut, water and coconut extract. Beat well.

Dredge each shrimp in the remainder 1 cup of flour. Holding the shrimp by the tail, dip in the batter mixture. Allow excess to drip off and roll in the remaining coconut.

Deep fry at 325° until golden brown (about three minutes). Serve immediately with the dipping sauce.

Dipping Sauce

Add the Grand Marnier to orange marmalade and mix well. Chill to thicken. Serve into hollowed out oranges for individual plate servings.

Midge Trubey

Kathy's Black Bean And Feta Dip

A crowd pleaser for that game-day TV party.

1 can of black beans, drained and rinsed

1 can of shoepeg corn, drained, do not rinse

1 bunch of scallions, sliced using white and green tops

8 oz of crumbled feta cheese, drained

<u>Mix all the above together, then make your dressing:</u>

¼ c apple cider vinegar

¼ c extra light olive oil (not extra virgin)

¼ c sugar or Splenda

Pour your dressing over your mixture, mixing well. Add salt, pepper and garlic powder to taste.

Serve with tostado scoops.

Janie's Rotiessierre Chicken Casserole

Janie made this for me when I had my hip replacement surgery, boy, was it delicious!

3 c of pulled rotisserie chicken cut in fork size bites

1 can of cream of chicken/celery/mushroom soup (Janie uses what she has on hand)

1 c of mayonnaise (Hellman's of course)

1 can sliced water chestnuts, do not drain

1 c sliced mushrooms - jar or fresh- again do not drain if using canned/jar)

1 package of frozen French green beans, defrosted, drain, do not precook

1 package of long and wild rice, cooked according to package directions

1 small jar pimentos (optional)

Mix well all the above and put into a 2-quart buttered casserole dish. Bake at 350° until it is bubbly.

Robin's Cheese Spread

Best to be served with a butter cracker. Delicious to drop on top of a baked potato and/or hot broccoli. To die for!! Enjoy!!

2 Blocks of Extra Sharp Cracker Barrel Cheese, grated

2 bunches scallions, chopping using the green stems also

1 can of black olives, drained and chopped

Hellman's Mayonnaise

Put the first three ingredients in a mixing bowl. Add Hellman's just enough to hold this mixture together. Mix well. Cover and refrigerate overnight or at least a few hours. Before serving, set out to get room temperature. Add more mayonnaise if needed to soften to stir. This spread needs to be served at room temperature.

Midge's Favorite Hot Artichoke Dip

One of my go-to party recipes; never any leftovers.

3 cans of artichokes, well drained and chop in food processor	2 c of Hellman's mayonnaise	1 c of parmesan cheese

Mix all three of these ingredients in a mixing bowl and put into a 1 ½-quart baking dish. Sprinkle more parmesan cheese on the top, enough to give an even thin top coating. Bake at 350° until dip is a nice golden color on the top. Serve with your butter cracker, Ritz or Triscuits.

Midge Trubey

Patricia's Buffalo Chicken Dip

This is a great one directly from my friend who says she cannot cook. I love it!

◇◇

2 large chicken breasts, cooked and shredded (for a short cut, use grocery deli rotisserie chicken)

2 - 8 oz. blocks of cream cheese, microwave until soft or room temperature

2/3 c chunky blue cheese

2/3 c hot sauce (Patricia uses Hooter's Hot Sauce)

2/3 c chopped celery, sautéed in butter until soft

◇◇

Mix all the ingredients together until well blended, put into baking dish. Bake at 350° for 20 minutes. Serve with tostado chips.

Reflections of
A "Rockin' Cook"

There are so many things that this incredible career has taught me, not only personally, but as the entrepreneur that I became. The first lesson is never, ever be late to a job. Whether you are an owner, manager or employee, be on time. That just needs no further explanation at all.

When you accept a job, there are never any excuses about not completing that job ever. The job is the job is the job period. With that in mind, you better have passion and excitement for your job under any and all conditions. Weather does not matter, nor the fact that you are not feeling well, no excuses.

If you take care of your job with a smile on your face, your job will take care of you. Put yourself into your work, and the rewards are staggering. The sense of accomplishment and pride with a job well done will give you such peace of mind and joy. Yes, you are probably tired, but it is a happy tired. In today's world, how about just having a job? You are adding experiences to your life with each passing day. Each day teaches you something new if you are receptive, whether you are working for yourself or for another. Learning is a great thing! No time for selfishness or a large ego. These character traits will get you in trouble every time when you are working for a customer or client. Find a reason to like what you are doing. Positive attitudes are always noticed.

Time is money, so which are you concentrating on? If you concentrate on the time and doing the complete job for your customer, the money will come. This is my belief. If you zero in on the money first, you will forget your purpose of time for your customer. If you take care of your time with your clients, they will rehire you and recommend you to other customers.

Speaking of money, does making a lot of money label you a success in business? I say no. Money is nice, don't get me wrong. Money is a necessity for life. You need money to buy or rent a home, pay the electric and water bills, and buy the groceries for yourself and your family. I do not believe that those with the most toys win in the game of life. It is what you do with your success that matters, not necessarily the fact that you have a lot of money in the bank. Success is also a feeling of well-being and accomplishment, and the fact that you are helping or assisting someone else. I believe your work is a part of your journey; it is not your life.

God gives you tools to use in your journey of life, and we all have different strengths and weaknesses. It is up to each of us to learn how to use our talents. I love to sing, but I cannot carry a note in a bucket. I love to dance, but I am definitely not graceful, nor can I carry a beat for long. My entertainers have reminded me of this on numerous occasions. I love to cook, but am I the best cook ever? Absolutely not. I can hold my own in the kitchen thanks to watching and learning from my mom, my grandmother, and my mother in law. God gave me a very creative mind and the thirst for learning. I tapped into those gifts and never looked back. I listened, cooked, prayed for solutions to whatever dilemmas were presented to me. The answers came, and I moved forward. I was motivated by the fact that I wanted to do something positive with my life, plus I had two precious children that were counting on me to provide for them.

I was, and still am, curious. I love to learn something new. After thirty years of working and managing my own company, retirement was handed to me. At that time, nothing was for sale, but my two business properties sold within 6 months of each other. Wow! I was retired! I helped my mom, wrote this book, and enjoyed having free time for the first time in my life.

There are no excuses for poor job performance, ever. Always be true to why you are working. If you are an entrepreneur, your time is never your own. You better have passion, determination, and devotion to creating your adventure. If you have passion for your job, you will never work a day in your life. When you own your own business, the days are never ever eight or ten hours of work. Forget working a five-day work week. The day is completed when the job is over, period. This makes developing a business so extremely difficult for spouses or partners, and particularly challenging for people with children. My children were little when I started The Personal Touch. My parents did not help me; they felt they had raised their own children and that it was my time to raise mine. I had to figure out my own way.

When I was traveling on the road, one-hundred dollar bills were like one-dollar bills; perspective and perception could change way too quickly. I always wanted to get home as fast as I could. I wanted to get back to cleaning my toilet, mowing the yard, taking my children to and from school, and going on school trips. Juggling a balance was so delicate. When I was not on the road, I played with my kids. They were my life. I always tried to do my paperwork or make my phone calls when my kids were at school. When school was over, we played at the parks and went to the beaches, all free things that living in Florida provided. In retrospect, I hope that I did a good job with my children and did not scar them for life! I know that I did the best I could. For the most part, the look backwards is kind filled, with lots of different stories depending on which one of us is telling that particular story. The three of us have a great sense of humor with each other. My adult children are my best friends.

Believe me, to have your own business is hard work, no matter what occupation you choose. Throughout my rock era, I would have people tell me how glamorous my life was and tell me how lucky I was to be traveling with all those famous people. Undoubtedly, these same people would go home to their nice homes with nice dinners and climb into their nice beds while I crawled onto the crew bus or into the trucks to find my little sleeping coffin. Are there sacrifices? You bet. Having your own business is no cake walk. I do not want to discourage you, but I want you to realize that running a business really takes dedication. You must believe in your idea with all your heart and soul. To run your own business is the experience of a lifetime, and the journey is awesome. Being a stay-at-home mom is running a business too. Think about it.

I tell my children to this day to believe in themselves. Believe in your inner self and gut feelings, and you cannot go wrong. There is no time for fear or indecision; you can do anything. Both of them are very happy to be working for other companies. Neither of them want to hurt my feelings with their opinions of not being a business owner. I totally understand how Melanie and Corbett feel. My children know we sacrificed time away from each other, but I feel like we made it together to the end as a strong family unit. I will always hope that I made the right decisions, but you can never go backwards. You make the best decisions at the time they are happening, move forward, then do not look backwards. A positive attitude is key to your sense of happiness and well-being. It is helpful to remember that life is bigger than you. Have a sense of humor, especially if you are feeling low. Laughter is great medicine and has proven to be a great stress reducer. The situation that has you feeling low is only a path of experience and life. Move forward.

I believe in the power of music for motivation, romance, healing, bringing mobs of people together in harmony, pure enjoyment, and reflecting in moments of sadness and protest. When you stand on a stage as I have, and see thousands, and I mean thousands, of people singing, dancing and swaying to the music, there are no wrongs or ills in the world at that moment. Music unites us, excites us, and relaxes us. Very rarely do you see an angry mob marching and burning to the sound of music. Artists can have a wonderful voice, a voice that you remember from years ago that is now faded, or an artist can have a talent with a musical instrument that can move you to the emotions of joy or crying. What a gift to share with the world.

Each artist has a crew behind them. This crew provides the lights and sound and support. They are the guts of each show. Back in the seventies, these crews were primarily men. Today, men and women work side-by-side on these diverse shows. These people are the unsung heroes of the traveling road. When something breaks down, repairs must be made very quickly, and usually on location. Remember, the show starts at 8 pm. Anything can happen as my stories have told you, but at 8 pm, all eyes are on the stage. Showtime.

To say the music business is challenging is an understatement. This work is adrenaline-pumping, mind-blowing, exhausting, and accelerating thrill to be part of. The rush of being involved in this type of work gets into your blood, just like the sand between your toes if you live near a beach. Many businesses have this thrill. How about the first pitch in a baseball season? Once you have experienced this thrill, you can never get that feeling out of your system. You are part of something bigger than yourself. It is creative passion in its finest form. There are two songs that immediately come to mind when thinking about life on the road: Bob Seger's "Turn the Page" and Willy Nelson's "On the Road Again." You need to listen to these songs! Enough said.

The goal of these traveling families is to pursue their love for the music, the rush, and the thrill. Eighteen-hour workdays day in and out are no picnic, but the passion for the finished product on stage is electrifying. Because of their dedication to their trade, the money comes. The entire crew, the artist, and the support staff are making money because of their passion.

When talking about the people that make these shows happen, you cannot forget to name the office personnel that work diligently behind their desks, day after day, securing venues, working on the riders, and handling the daily crisis, whatever it might be. These people, for the most part, do not travel, but the road could not operate without their daily support.

With the 2020 pandemic, the music/touring business is changing as social distancing at a music gathering is virtually impossible. I believe these creative people will find a way to share their talents and music. I wish I were not retired so that I could be part of this new solution of ideas. "We Are the World" will rise again. for solutions.

When you are receptive to the gifts of each day, the adventures of life can take you beyond your wildest dreams. The ride can be like a roller coaster, slow, fast, up, down, and even some side motion. Running your own company is not for the faint of heart. "Hold your tummy," as my mom would say. I changed her phrase to "Grab your ass with both hands. It's going to be a bumpy ride." You can never have tunnel vision when running your company. I think of tunnel vision as the horse that quietly pulls the carriage in the park with blinders on the sides of his head. They keep his eyes focused on only what is in front of him. He is great at moving forward, slow and steady, but this horse cannot see what is happening on either side of him. When moving your company through its life cycle, you must know what is happening in your surroundings, not only in front of you, but to your left and to your right. Never ever forget where you came from, but keep moving. You must listen to what your customers are telling you, their wants and their needs, and you must adapt. Your business must become like that river, rambling left and right, over the rocks and waterfalls, but steadily moving forwards. Exciting times await you if you pay attention.

Your company is not only you but also about the people that come along with you on your journey. Your family. Your employees that believe in you. Your customers that are counting on you for that party, that wedding, that corporate meeting. Consideration for these people is paramount to success, both personal and business. Will you make mistakes? You bet. Will you have sleepless nights? Absolutely! Will you be tired? No question, yes. But you can claim your success by listening, adapting, and always moving forward with the ideas that started you on your journey in the first place. Talk to people, ask questions, and do lots of research before you start your company. I want to encourage you to find your niche in business. Be the best that you can be. It is OK to reach for the stars!

You will have an education each day, the college of hard knocks. After reading this, I think I should have a doctorate by now. (Just joking.) But I have learned so much. I know that I have had the time of my life. I have tried to be true to myself and to my children, family, employees, and customers all along the way. My customers have been everyday people as well as some of the most talented and creative artists in the world. God gave these artists talents that have inspired so many people through generations. To be involved with their music has totally been the biggest adventure.

I want to inspire you to be better at whatever you do. Whatever business you do, it must become a part of you. Feel it, know it, and have no fear about what you can accomplish. Know your strengths as well as your weakness. What skills or knowledge you don't have, make sure you hire someone that can have your back in that particular area. Know your community, and ask people what is needed to make it a better place to live. How can you develop in that area? Always use the "three P's" of business: Proper Prior Planning. Also remember the KISS strategy: Keep It Simple Stupid. No disrespect intended. You must have a sense of humor about yourself, and never let your ego get in the way. You are creating your own classroom of business. Do not trip yourself up with complications. Your customers will add complications of their own without your help. If you stay sharp with your goals in mind, you will be ready to help your customers with their last-minute dramas. Then you can shine in assisting them. I lost count of the number of times I was sent to the grocery store for last-minute requests from various artists and crew. I would put a smile on my face and say "no problem" as I ran out the door to the store. Was I always happy to be pulled in another direction? No. The trick was that I had to be organized, anticipating that last minute request, so when that out-of-the-blue request came, it was a mere bump in the road, and not a train wreck. Organization and staying ahead is always key to a successful project. Of course, I always smiled.

When working with food, you can only stay so far ahead so that you serve the quality of food that makes your name. So much goes into the preparation and presentation of food. I say to this day, "food does not just hop onto a plate." In the late 70s and 80s, we did not have all the famous chefs with their television shows to inspire us. We did have Julia Child, but you certainly did not have the time on the road to cook like that! The key to cooking in those days was ease, simplicity, and good quality. For me today, the key to cooking is the exact same: ease, simplicity, and good quality. I wish I had had some of the recipes that I love today way back then! I have learned much in the years after the road. I love sharing this knowledge to all who are interested.

I can never ever give enough thank-yous to all the people that made my journey, "Mr. Toad's Wild Ride," such a grand adventure. One big thank you will have to do for everyone who ever lived the life of the road, both artists and crew, the ones I worked for and lived with, and write about in this book. You inspired me in so many ways to keep going. Thank you. Another big round of thanks is due to all the employees that believed in me and gave their dedication and time to the various departments of The Personal Touch. I valued your time, your thoughts, and your help. None of this would have been possible without you all. Thank you, family, for believing in me. So many of you worked tirelessly, especially my sister Alice. I love each of you dearly. And friends. Where would we be without them? I must single out a few that without their help and encouragement, this book would not have been completed: Joyce Moore, Kate Harold, Judy Duggan, Bill Gatzemos, Crystal Gayle, Dr. Mary Guthrie, Susie Shuck, Kathy McDole, James Walker, Chad Zook, Roy Peter Clark, Amy Cianci, The St. Petersburg Press. And Kenny Rogers, a huge thank you.

To all of my clients and customers that came to The Personal Touch for help in our over 30 years of business, I thank you all for the catering, flowers, weddings, meetings and parties. Your prom corsage was as important as your bridal bouquet. Your backyard barbecue was as important as your wedding day. Your business meeting was as important as that grand Christmas party at Mansion by The Bay. Feeding your children at the many schools was so important, no child ever went hungry. I valued all of you then and I value the friendships that have remained throughout all these years. All of you made The Personal Touch a grand memory for me. It is my hope that you have good memories also. I was always striving to be the best that I could be.

Last but definitely not least, I want to thank my children, Melanie and Corbett. Both of you have indulged me by fact checking this book several times before printing. I actually wanted to make sure that I was not embarrassing you two, as I have been known to do. Hey, I'm a mom! You two have always been my joy. You two are my heart and soul. Bless your hearts for being with me on my adventures, and actually smiling and laughing most of the time! Thank you to God for your protection and guidance. You were the biggest mentor of all. To wake up in the mornings, to have the answers to so many questions that were on my plate answered from the night before, was true inspiration.

I think it is time for me to get a rocking chair with a jet pack on the back for intense rocking power with custom built-in speakers! Maybe while I am rocking and grooving, a new idea might come to me? For the rest of you, "Rock On," and thanks for listening to my stories!

Midge Trubey

Corbet Trubey, Midge Trubey
& Melanie Trubey Doooley,
"We Survived!"

Sweet Endings

You cannot have a good meal without great endings, by this I mean desserts. Here are some favorite dessert recipes from family, friends and my personal collection.

Aunt Betty Jane's Fruit Slices Breakfast Bread

I always smiled when my aunt walked in the door with this one!

1 c butter

4 eggs, room temperature

1 ¾ c sugar

3 c sifted flour

1 tsp vanilla

1 ½ tsp baking powder

1 can prepared pie filling, your choice of "flavors"

½ tsp salt

Cream butter, sugar and vanilla. Add the eggs one at a time, making sure well blended. Sift flour, baking powder and salt together in another bowl. Add to the creamed mixture. Spread batter in greased 13×9 baking dish, saving 1 ¼ cups for the last step. Drop your pie filling by the teaspoon on top of your batter. Drop your remainder saved batter by the teaspoon on top of your pie filling.

Bake 35-45 minutes in a 350° oven. Down when the toothpick inserted comes out clean, do not overcook. Cool and sprinkle with confectioners' sugar.

Midge Trubey

Midge's Gift Breads

The next three recipes, banana bread, pumpkin bread and zucchini bread, I would make at the holidays to sell in my flower shop as gifts.

Banana Nut Bread

½ c butter

1 c sugar

1 egg

3 large, mashed bananas, over ripe a must

½ c walnuts (optional)

½ tsp salt

1 tsp baking powder

1 tsp baking soda (dissolve in buttermilk)

2/3 c buttermilk

2 c flour

Cream butter and sugar. Add the other ingredients in order. Grease loaf pan on the sides and wax paper the bottom. Bake 40-50 minutes at 350°

Pumpkin Bread

1 1/3 c sugar

½ c oil, I use Wesson or Crisco

¼ tsp baking powder

½ tsp salt

½ tsp cinnamon

½ tsp nutmeg

½ tsp cloves

1 2/3 c flour

1 tsp baking soda

1 c can pumpkin

1 c chopped nuts or raisins (optional)

Mix all ingredients and bake in loaf pan at 350° for 45-55 minutes. Sprinkle too with powdered sugar as it is coming out of the oven (optional)

Midge Trubey

Zucchini Bread

3 tbsp butter, softened

1 c sugar

2 large eggs at room temperature

1 tbsp grated orange rind

1 - 16 oz can whole cranberry sauce

1 ½ c un-sifted whole wheat flour

1 ½ c un-sifted all-purpose flour

1 tsp baking soda

1 ½ c coarsely grated zucchini

1 c chopped walnuts (optional)

Cream butter, sugar and eggs until fluffy. Stir in orange rind and cranberry sauce. Sift the two flours together along with the baking soda and baking powder. Add these to the butter mixture, fold in until just combined. Fold in zucchini and walnuts. Turn into greased loaf pan with waxes papered bottom. Bake 350° oven for about one hour. Do not overcook, this is a moist dense bread.

Cousin Barbara's
Lemon Lush Dessert

Getting this family recipe from Ohio was so very special.

◇◇◇

1 c flour

½ c (1 stick) butter, softened

1 c chopped pecans (optional)

1 - 8 oz cream cheese, softened

1 c powdered sugar

1 - 9 oz container of cool whip

2 packages instant lemon pudding

3 c whole milk

◇◇◇

Mix flour, butter and pecans. Press into 9x13 pan, lightly greased. Bake 25 minutes at 325° Cool.

Mix cream cheese, sugar and 1 cup cool whip. Spread over crust. Mix pudding and milk. Spread over mixture. Top with remaining cool whip. Garnish with nuts or well drained chopped cherries or zest of a fresh lemon. Refrigerate.

Midge Trubey

Grandmother Muriel Trubey's Banana Cake

This is a cherished family recipe. My son made this and used chocolate icing.

◇◇

2 ½ c flour

2 ½ tsp baking powder

½ tsp baking soda

½ tsp salt

½ c shortening, Crisco

1 ¼ c sugar

2 eggs, separated

1 ½ tsp vanilla

¼ c whole milk

1 c mashed ripe banana

½ c coconut or ½ c walnuts or ½ c combo
(optional)

◇◇

Mix dry ingredients. Cream shortening and sugar: add egg yolks, vanilla, milk, bananas, stir just to blend. Fold in egg whites that you have beaten stiff.

Bake at 375° in a greased and floured 9x13 pan for 25 minutes or until toothpick inserted comes away clean.

Mrs. Reeves Secret, Famous Carrot Cake

I had to beg and plead to get this recipe back in 1968.

2 c sugar	½ tsp salt	1 ½ c Wesson oil
4 eggs, room temperature	2 tsp baking powder	3 c grated carrots
1 ½ c flour	2 tsp cinnamon	1 c chopped walnuts
2 tsp baking soda		

Beat eggs into sugar one at a time. Add dry ingredients that have been sifted together. Add oil to mixture a little at a time. Add carrots and nuts. Pour into three 8-inch cake pans that are greased and lined with wax paper. Bake at 350° for 25-30 minutes. When cakes are cooled, take out of pans.

Frosting

I have been known to double this as I like FROSTING

½c (1 stick) of butter	¾ to 1 box 10X powdered sugar (sweeten to taste)	2 tsp vanilla
8 oz cream cheese		

Naturally, blend until smooth and creamy.

Midge Trubey

187

Mrs. K's 7-Up Cake

I picked up this recipe when I was a Tupperware lady in the early 70s.

◇◇

1 ½ c butter	5 eggs, room temperature	2 tbsp fresh lemon juice
3 c sugar	3 c flour	3 ¼ c 7 Up

◇◇

Cream sugar and butter together, beat until light and fluffy. Add eggs one at a time. Add lemon juice and 7 Up, mix until well blended. Pour batter into well-greased and floured jumbo fluted mold. Bake at 325° for 1 -1 ¼ hour or until toothpick comes clean. Sprinkle with powdered sugar.

Pat Trubey's Orange Cupcakes

A favorite of my children when they were growing up.

<><><><><><><><><><><><><><><><><><><><><><><><><><><><><><>

**Sift together
in a bowl**

1 ¼ c flour

**2 tsp baking
powder**

¾ c sugar

¼ tsp salt

**1 egg unbeaten,
room temperature**

**¼ c margarine
or butter, room
temperature**

**¼ c Pet milk (evap-
orated)**

¼ c orange juice

<><><><><><><><><><><><><><><><><><><><><><><><><><><><><><>

Add the above 4 ingredients to your sifted flour. Beat 2-3 minutes until blended. Bake at 350° 15-20 minutes or until done. Makes about 14 2-inch cupcakes.

Orange Frosting

I have been known to double this as I like FROSTING

<><><><><><><><><><><><><><><><><><><><><><><><><><><><><><>

**1 to 1 1/3 c 10X
powdered sugar
(sweeten to taste)**

**¾ tsp grated or-
ange rind**

Dash of salt

**Milk (about 2 tbsp,
may need to add
more)**

<><><><><><><><><><><><><><><><><><><><><><><><><><><><><><>

Beat all the above until smooth.

Midge Trubey

Pat Trubey's Chocolate Cake

A favorite recipe from my Mother-in-Law, everyone loves this!

◇◇

2 c flour

2 c sugar

2 c hot black coffee

1 c cocoa

2 tsp vanilla

1 tsp salt

2 tsp baking soda, dissolved in the

hot coffee

½ c canned Crisco

◇◇

Cream sugar and Crisco. Mix together the flour, cocoa and salt, add to the sugar mixture alternating with the coffee. Begin and end with the flour mixture. Blend in vanilla. Bake in greased 9x13 pan about 30 minutes 350°at or until the toothpick comes out clean. Do not overcook.

Midge's Apple Cake

I love this warm with vanilla ice cream. The best! Good for snacking.

~~~~~~

2 ½ c all-purpose flour

2 tsp baking powder

1 tsp baking soda

¾ tsp salt

1 c (2 sticks) of margarine (not butter)

2 eggs, room temperature

2 c sugar

3 c chopped apples

¾ c chopped walnut or pecans (optional)

~~~~~~

Sift all dry ingredients together. Set aside. Cream margarine, add sugar, beat. Add eggs one at a time, beat. Add the dry ingredients, mix well. Add the apples and nuts, folding into batter. Batter will be thick. Spoon into greased and floured 13×9 pan. Bake 350° for one hour or nice golden-brown top, do not overcook.

Glaze for cake

~~~~~~

1 c 10X powdered sugar

1 tbsp margarine

1 tbsp whole milk

1 tbsp Karo syrup

~~~~~~

Mix together and put on cake while cake is warm.

Midge Trubey

Yummy Molasses Cookies

What sold me on this recipe is that the cookies stay soft!

◇◇

1 ½ c (3 sticks) butter, softened

2 c sugar

2 eggs, room temperature

½ c molasses

4 ½ c all-purpose flour

4 tsp ground ginger

2 tsp baking soda

1 ½ tsp ground cinnamon

1 tsp ground cloves

¼ tsp salt

¼ c chopped pecans (can be omitted, I like them without nuts)

¼ c coarse or regular sugar, your choice (I use regular)

◇◇

In a large bowl, cream butter and sugar until light and fluffy. Beat in eggs and molasses. Combine the flour, ginger, baking soda, cinnamon, cloves and salt. Gradually add to creamed mixture and mix well. Add pecans at this point, if using.

Shape into one inch. Balls and roll in sugar. Place about 2 inches apart on ungreased baking sheets. Bake at 400° for about 15 minutes or until tops are cracked, do not overcook. Remove to wire rack to cool.

Janie's Lacey Cookies

My girlfriend would bring these cookies to my home for Christmas parties. Always a hit!

◇◇

½ c (1 stick) of butter

1 c granulated sugar

1 ½ c Quaker oats (can be original or quick)

1 beaten egg, room temperature

1 tsp vanilla

◇◇

Melt butter in saucepan, mix in sugar, remove from heat. All other ingredients and mix together. Cover your cookie sheet with aluminum foil, shiny side up. Spoon onto foil. Bake at 350° for 10 minutes or until the edges are brown. Let cookies cool and then you can peel them off foil. Makes about 3 dozen cookies. You do not want cookies to be very large, used about ½ teaspoon, two inches apart.

Midge Truby

Picnic Dump Cake

Need something quick for dessert? Here it is. Hot at home with vanilla ice cream on top is a winner!

---

1 - 20 oz can crushed pineapple, undrained

1 - 21 oz can cherry pie filling

1 standard boxed yellow cake mix

1 c chopped pecans

½ c (1 stick) of butter, cut in thin slices

Lightly grease 9x13 pan and dump the above ingredients in the order given. The thinly sliced butter pats should be placed on the top.

Bake at 350° for one hour. Serve warm and Enjoy!! Serve with vanilla ice cream or fresh whipped cream or Cool Whip.

Peanut Butter Kiss Cookies

Very rich! My niece, Lori, and her daughter Kristen,
make these for Christmas every year.

1 c peanut butter (do not use reduced fat peanut butter)	1 c sugar	1 tsp vanilla extract
	1 egg, room temperature	24 Hershey Kisses

In a large bowl, cream peanut butter and sugar until light and fluffy. Add the egg and vanilla beat until ingredients are blended.

Roll into 1 ¼-inch balls. Place 2 inches apart on ungreased baking sheets. Bake at 350° for 10-12 minutes or until tops are slightly cracked.

Immediately on pulling out of the oven, press chocolate kiss into the center of each cookie. Let cool for 5 minutes before removing from pans to wire racks.

Midge Trubey

Midge's Yummy Chocolate Pie

This one is another huge favorite of my children when they were growing up.

◇◇

½ c (1 stick) of butter

1 square unsweetened chocolate (in your baking section)

1 c granulated sugar

2 whole eggs, beaten, room temperature

1 tsp vanilla

Dash of salt

1 frozen 9-inch pie crust

◇◇

Melt butter and chocolate square in a double boiler over low heat (small pan sitting in large pan with hot water on your burner, do not let water into your little pan). Pour hot chocolate and butter over sugar in another bowl. Add 2 beaten eggs, stir, add dash of salt and vanilla, stir. Pour into frozen pie crust. Bake at 350° for 30 minutes, let sit up for about 15 minutes. Serve warm with vanilla ice cream. I must tell you a story about this recipe.

I say it is mine, but a young Mom (as myself) in Winston Salem, NC gave me this recipe back in 1977, I do not remember her name!! I have made this recipe all these years.

Grandmother Herden's Bourbon Balls

Truth be known, Grandmother would sometimes use this same recipe with rum instead!! We all grew up loving these!!
Still a family favorite.

◇◇◇

1 - 12 oz package vanilla waters, finely crushed

1 c chopped pecans, toasted (can be omitted)

¾ c 10X powdered sugar

2 tbsp unsweetened cocoa

½ c bourbon (or rum)

1 ½ tbsp light corn syrup

Additional p owdered sugar to roll your "balls" in

◇◇◇

Stir together the first four ingredients in a large stainless-steel bowl until well blended.

Stir together bourbon and corn syrup until well blended. Add bourbon mixture to wafer mixture, stir until blended. Mixture will be rather gooey, do not worry, this is correct. Put your stainless-steel bowl into the refrigerator to chill the mixture. Shape cold mixture into 1-inch balls and roll in additional powdered sugar. Place balls into airtight storage container lined with waxed paper. You can stack the balls in the container using wax paper between the layers so that they will not stick together. Cover and chill for up to two weeks. Grandmother always said they taste better after they had "sat" for a while.

Midge Trubey

Marnie's Pretzel Dessert

It is fun to watch your guests trying to figure out what the crust is made of! Who would guess?

◇◇

Crust:	First layer:	Second layer:
1 ½ c crusted pretzels (not fine)	1 - 8oz pkg of cream cheese	2 - 3oz. pkg Strawberry Jell-O
½ c melted butter	1 large carton Cool Whip	2 c boiling water
½ c sugar (or Splenda)	1 c sugar (or Splenda)	1 qt freshly sliced strawberries or 2 pkg. frozen strawberries

◇◇

Prepare the crust and gently press into a 9 x 13 inch gently greased pan to be the crust of your dish. Bake at 325° for 6 minutes. Cool.

First layer: Combine ingredients and whip until fluffy. Pour over the crust and refrigerate.

Second layer: Mix your strawberry Jell -O and boiling water first then add your strawberries. If using fresh strawberries, let your mixture start to set up in the refrigerator before you pour it on top of your first layer. If you are using frozen strawberries, the frozen berries will hasten this chilling process and the mixture can go on the top sooner. When the second layer is complete, refrigerate your entire dish until serving time.

Grandson Christian's Healthy Smoothie

My grandson, Christian, makes this at home for his healthy snack. I think he's trying to teach me new tricks.

∞∞∞∞∞∞∞∞∞∞∞∞∞∞∞∞∞∞∞∞∞∞∞∞∞∞∞∞∞∞∞∞∞∞∞∞

In your blender, put about 1 c of crushed ice.

3 tsp vanilla extract

1-2 c Any fresh fruit that you desire

2 tbsp of honey

Juice of one wedge of lime

2 - 6 oz containers of yogurt, any flavor, Christian likes vanilla

1-2 c milk, pour on top

∞∞∞∞∞∞∞∞∞∞∞∞∞∞∞∞∞∞∞∞∞∞∞∞∞∞∞∞∞∞∞∞∞∞∞∞

Turn your blender on until all ice is thoroughly crushed and smooth. This is delicious. I am proud of him for sharing his healthy snack, I keep the blender in the frig until it is gone, and I start again with a "new creation" of flavors.

Cook Onward & Rock On!!

Alice backstage with breakfast

Dire Straits, Peter Cashman, just for you

Donny Osmond

Backstage food set up

1979 Crew Tour Pass, Journey

Having fun backstage

Entertainers We Fed

Backstage during Spring Break

Michael Jackson and 2 of his brothers, St. Petersburg, FL

Filming the movie "Health" with Robert Altman on St. Pete Beach

A very young Ozzy Osbourne coming in from a secret fishing trip that I arranged

Midge and alligator, Barbara Tucker, theme party for Southland Corporation, Orlando, Florida

Midge and Cheryl and ELP crew in the Bahamas on dinner break from Love Beach recording

Midge Trubey

About the Author

Midge Trubey is a Florida-based entrepreneur and business owner with over 30 years in the hospitality industry. In 1977 she founded The Personal Touch, a catering company that grew to include a flower shop, banquet halls, school lunch program, and nationwide corporate and convention coordinating services. She's been recognized by multiple organizations as a finalist for the Small Businessperson of the Year, and her company has been awarded several times as a favorite service throughout the Tampa Bay area. She's also been featured on national news shows, newspapers, and leading trade publications. In 2007 she retired, and now happily resides in St. Petersburg, her hometown since birth.

If you would like to see the author in action, follow this link below to watch her 1981 interview with Maria Shriver.

https://www.youtube.com/watch?v=s3WhlE9oeLQ

Entertainers We Fed

Measurement	Abbreviation
teaspoon	tsp
tablespoon	tbsp
fluid ounce	fl oz
cup	c
pint	pt
quart	qt
gallon	gal
pound	lb
ounce	oz

Made in United States
North Haven, CT
03 October 2022

24820498R00113